PEOPLES OF ROMAN BRITAIN

General Editor Keith Branigan
Lecturer in Archaeology in the University of Bristol

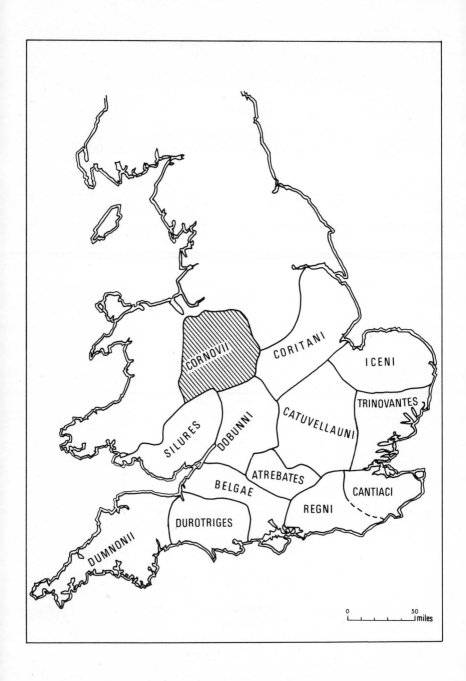

THE

CORNOVII

GRAHAM WEBSTER
Reader in Romano-British Archaeology
in the University of Birmingham

DUCKWORTH

First published in 1975 by
Gerald Duckworth and Co. Ltd.
43 Gloucester Crescent,
London, NW1

Cloth ISBN 7156 0832 0
Paper ISBN 7156 0833 9

Typeset in Great Britain by
Specialised Offset Services Ltd., Liverpool,
and printed by
Unwin Brothers Ltd., Old Woking

Contents

Acknowledgments

This brief account of the Cornovii would not have been possible without the help of several colleagues, field workers and excavators who have generously given me information and ideas and allowed me to use the results of their work, often in advance of their own publication. I am especially indebted to Philip Barker, Dr. Stan Stanford, Geoffrey Toms, Ernie Jenks, Dr. J. Houghton, John Pagett, Mrs. Joan Miller, Arnold Baker and Miss L.F. Chitty; also to Brian Hartley, Donald Mackreth, Mark Hassell, Professor Kenneth Jackson, Dr. Peter Toghill, John Wacher, Mrs Sonia Hawkes, Professor David Wilson, Trevor Rowley and Dr. John Mann for advice on specific points. I am grateful for permission to use photographs to Professor J.K. St. Joseph and the Committee for Aerial Photography, The University of Cambridge, to John Hampton and the Royal Commission on Historical Monuments (England) and to the Ilkley Urban District Council.

List of illustrations

Line drawings by Jennifer Gill

To Lily F. Chitty
for life-long dedication to the archaeology
of the Welsh Marches and her unstinted
generosity to all students who come
to her for help

1.

Tribal Territory and the Pre-Roman Iron Age

The county of Shropshire has one of the most interesting and varied landscapes of any in Britain and this is due to the contrasts between the old rocks of the palaeozoic sequence, which stand up in rugged grandeur, their hardness having made them resistant to time's eroding agencies, and the softer rocks of more recent geological times, mainly the red sandstone of the Triassic series. Much of the area, especially to the south-west, is hill country, an extension of the Welsh uplands, but breaking through here and there with dramatic impact on the scenery are the volcanic intrusions like the Wrekin and the Clees. The northern area is an extensive plain covered by glacial drift with its mixtures of gravel, sand and boulder clay (fig. 1), in places covering the underlying rocks to a thickness of 45 metres. This is broken by red sandstone ridges running in a north-easterly direction from Nesscliffe to Hawkestone, which has produced over the Shropshire Plain very differing conditions for human settlement and cultivation. In some places there are lakes and great bogs, residues of meltwaters dammed up at the end of the Ice Age, which formed Lake Lapworth, waters from which spilled out with such pressure that they carved out the Ironbridge gap and created the present course of the Severn.[1] In spite of recent drainage, a large number of meres and pools in the north-western part of the county between the Dee and the Severn can still be seen on the one-inch map. These swamps would have been very attractive to the indigenous peoples of the Middle and Late Bronze Age since they could retreat there from the new, powerful Iron Age folk pressing steadily from

Fig. 1. The drift geology of the Wroxeter region

sands and gravels   sandstones   towns

Shrewsbury

Wroxeter

R. Severn

0   5   10 kms

the south. Fish and fowl were in plenty and the knowledge of the ways across the marshes would render them safe from sudden attack. The only traces of these peoples are their dug-out canoes,[2] net sinkers, bone harpoons and mounds of pot-boilers, but eventually their habitation sites will be found and studied. The waterlogged deposits which must exist will help to preserve many objects of wood, leather and textile which are normally lost and there may be good opportunities to discover much more about these early Cornovians.

The large areas of sand and gravel would have been covered with a light scrub and easily cleared for cultivation. Unfortunately, so little has been found that the extent of agriculture north of Shrewsbury cannot be assessed, but it would indeed be strange if there was a large blank on the map. The scatter of prehistoric finds may be thin, but it is evenly spread and must indicate settlement over much of the area. One of the odd things about Shropshire has been the number and size of the Bronze Age hoards of metalwork, and there has been a tendency to see this, as also the distribution of earlier stone implements, as the result of losses along trade routes.[3] One could not deny the importance of these routes which brought the stone implements from their factories in North Wales and Cumbria into the Midlands and beyond, but the hoards do suggest, perhaps, the presence of bronze-smiths working for a settled population. There is certainly no doubt about the richness of early settlement in the south of the country, brought out in dramatic form by Miss L.F. Chitty,[4] and this is in the hill country of a largely pastoral society. The discovery and excavation of the Middle Bronze Age cemeteries at Bromfield by Dr. Stanford[5] has underlined the importance of this area, and it must here surely be associated with the light and cultivable subsoils.

The most important physical feature which dominates the whole span of human movement and settlement is the River Severn, one of Britain's greatest rivers. Rising in the central mountain mass of Wales, it flows in a north-easterly direction, turning eastwards before it reaches Shrewsbury, and then to the south-east; and at the Ironbridge gap, its post-glacial course[6] flows almost directly south towards the Bristol Channel. The river was one of the main communi-

Fig. 2.   A view along the Wenlock Edge

cation routes and a source of food, since until quite recent times it teemed with salmon and other fish. Above all, it has a strategical aspect in providing easy access into central Wales and is large enough to have key crossing places where it could be forded or where ferries could be maintained. These controlled the east-west routes and made places like Worcester so significant throughout all periods.[7] Another crucial crossing place was at Bewdley where the Clun-Clee ridgeway reaches the river after coming over Titterstone Clee.[8] Miss Chitty has also drawn attention to the prehistoric finds linked with a crossing at Buildwas, a route which would have connected the Wrekin with sites to the south by means of a ridgeway along Wenlock Edge (fig. 2).[9] At Shrewsbury the marshes and the great bends of the Severn would have made crossings difficult and it is hardly surprising that the Roman road, which often followed earlier trackways, crossed well south of the site of the later town. Watling Street continued north of the Roman city over the Tern and through Attingham Park, and the crossing point must have been not far to the west of Atcham Bridge, the point Telford chose for his bridge. The road can then be postulated through Meole Brace, where it crossed the Rea Brook[10] and proceeded directly westwards towards the Welsh foothills. The relationship between this route and the Iron Age farms at Weeping Cross and Sharpstones Hill suggests that the Roman road may have been following an earlier trackway. It is difficult to reconstruct any other pre-Roman routes in the Shrewsbury area, but finds do suggest one from the north, perhaps crossing the Isle of Coton and fording the river near the later castle.

The Tribe

There are as yet no characteristics which help to isolate the tribe of the Cornovii from their neighbours. Unlike the tribes to the south-east, they had no coinage and all the British coins found in their territory were almost certainly brought there by Roman soldiers. Nor is there any distinctive metalwork; the finds have been very small in number and poor in quality. One turns hopefully to the pottery which

Fig. 3. The north face of the inturned entrance at the Iron Age hill-fort at The Roveries

elsewhere in Britain has features which enable some cultural affinities to be noted. But here too, the material offers little on which to base any useful conclusions. The work done by Dr. D.P.S. Peacock[11] and Dr. S.C. Stanford[12] suggests that the tribe belonged to a much larger grouping, since petrological examination of three main basic types of Iron Age pottery from Herefordshire and Shropshire indicates that much of it was made in the Malvern Hills. A small group of specialist potters was working here and distributing its wares over the whole of the Welsh Marches, including sites in Cornovian territory such as The Berth and the Breidden. This is in agreement with the broad concept of Professor Hawkes, as his Western Third B, postulated in 1958[13] and to which Dr. Stanford has added Western (Marches hill-fort) Fourth B[14] for the final phase at Credenhill, but it may be better to consider the whole simply as a Western Marches hill-fort culture. Such evidence as there is for the pottery and the structual details of sensitive features like defensive gateways (fig. 3) all point to a cultural entity on both sides of the Severn, including its upper reaches[15] and tributaries, and linked with the hill-forts to the south in the valley of the Wye. The differences between these citadels are due not to cultural differences but to chronological developments.

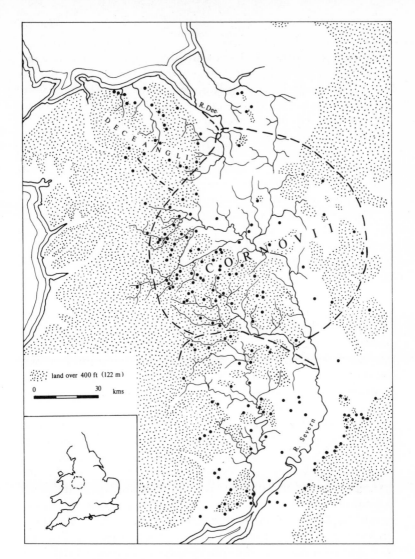

Fig. 4.   The distribution of hill-forts in the Cornovian canton

Using two great watersheds and the grouping of the hill-forts as a guide, it may be possible to indicate the areas of the two main peoples, the northern half of which appears to comprise the Cornovii (fig. 4). This corresponds closely with the ideas of Dr. Stanford in his discussion on the function of Credenhill Camp as the capital of the Herefordshire group,[16]

although it is difficult to accept his suggestion of the name
Decangi for these people, since the only other reference to
them, although in a post-Roman context, is Degannwy in
Caernarvonshire.[17] Whatever loyalties or obligations linked
the peoples of these areas, they were probably those of a
common ethnic origin prior to their migration to Britain.
There must have been a mixed population, the newcomers
with their superior weapons establishing a dominance over
the backward peasantry and each kind of feudal baron
carving out his territory, as Dr. Stanford's map suggests.[18]

If the size and massive character of the hill-forts (figs. 5,
6) give any indication of their relative importance, those
which stand out in Cornovian territory are Titterstone Clee,
Chesterton Walls and Bury Walls. Only at the first of these
has any excavation taken place and that was as long ago as
1932.[19] The unusual factor about this hill-fort is its
exceptional size of 71 acres (28 ha.). It commanded the Clee
Hills and the approach to the Severn Valley from the
south-east. At the time of excavation, almost the whole of
the south side had been destroyed by quarrying and landslip.
The work was concentrated on the defences, the bank and
entrance, and it may not be altogether surprising that no
pottery was found and the only metal object recorded is a
Saxon spear-head. The single line of defences, although much
eroded, was shown to have been quite formidable and of at
least two periods. The entrance on the south-side was
examined in detail and three periods were found with
evidence of destruction by fire. In the third period, guard
chambers were constructed on each side, a feature generally
dated by Dr. Stanford to the period 300-200 B.C., and there
is no evidence that this hill-fort continued its occupation into
the late Iron Age. Of the other massive hill-forts, Bury Walls
and Chesterton Walls, nothing is known, unfortunately. The
only Cornovian sites which have received any serious attention are the Wrekin and Caynham Camp. The former is a
great hog-back hill rising steeply almost a thousand feet
above the plain; the Celtic name must have been transferred
to Viroconium (below, p.17).

The excavations on the Wrekin were undertaken by Miss
Kathleen Kenyon in 1939 but only the first season was

Fig. 5.   The Iron Age hill-fort of Caer Caradoc, near Church Stretton

completed,[20] further work being prevented by the outbreak of the war. The hard volcanic rock can only be extracted in digging the ditches with great effort and the summit and windswept ridges would not present a very warm or comfortable residence. The people who constructed these defences and actually lived here must have placed security above everything else. The defences were found to have two main periods and there was evidence of post-holes and pits which showed that the interior was occupied. This has been confirmed recently by Dr. Stanford who undertook work there in advance of the construction of a television transmitting station, its approach road and other ancillary work. He found post-holes arranged in groups of four, forming squares, which are now generally accepted as the part of a house plan.[21] Another important conclusion reached by Dr. Stanford is that the buildings were finally destroyed by fire and it may be possible to decide by C14 dating whether this action belongs to the Roman conquest. The finds from these excavations have been remarkable only for their paucity; the pottery is lacking in character, but a short length of decorated bronze binding published by Miss Kenyon may have been from a scabbard-edging.

The excavations by Mr. Gelling at Caynham Camp, near Ludlow, have also proved to be somewhat inconclusive,[22] although there was ample evidence of buildings in the central area in the form of the large number of post-holes found. However, apart from one example (Site F), it proved impossible to organise them into hut plans. The first season's work produced four sherds of pottery and in the second, in spite of the inclusion of an area of buildings, the sherds were 'small and insignificant', totalling twenty-five altogether. These have been subjected to petrological analysis by Dr. Peacock.[23] Only three offer any identification of the source of the tempering and these come from the Clee Hills and Caynham is thus exceptional in not producing any Malvernian wares.

A hill-fort which could be claimed as within Cornovian territory is the Breiddin. An excavation was done here in 1933-5 by B.H. St. J. O'Neil[24] and more recently and more intensively by Mr. C. Musson. The full implication of their results will undoubtedly be more helpful than most of the other hill-fort investigations. A brief interim[25] has shown that the buildings inside the hill-fort fall into very distinct types. The earlier are rectangular houses associated with Malvernian pottery, and the later circular huts with wattle

Fig. 6.   The Iron Age hill-fort of Wall Hills, near Thornbury, Hereford-shire

walls associated with a much coarser type of pottery: the first chronological pattern to emerge which is different from that now established by Dr. Stanford in Herefordshire.[26]

Thus the Cornovian hill-forts contrast very strikingly with those of Herefordshire in the very meagre quantity of pottery and metalwork. This may be due to the choice of areas excavated, but it now seems more likely that the northern peoples were that much poorer in material resources. Caynham did at least produce a quantity of carbonised wheat grains, which suggests some dependance on arable farming. It is unfortunate that the extensive excavations, before the war, at Old Oswestry, one of the largest of the Cornovian hill-forts, have not been published, except in summary form.[27] The excavator, Professor W.J. Varley, records finding 'vast quantities of pottery which for the most part is quite revolting and indeed is virtually undistinguishable from the Eddisbury material'. There are, however, finer wares. He associated this material with the post-Roman period, but it

Fig. 7. Earthworks on the Long Mynd, Shrops., including early field systems

has been recognised by Dr. Stanford and Mr. Gelling as bearing a striking resemblance to what they have called 'very coarse pottery' or VCP, which they plausibly identified as fragments of small ovens of the Iron Age.[28] The widespread occurrence of similar fragments, now identified on fourteen sites, apart from Old Oswestry, establishes another link in this period which may not offer any suggestions of a cultural unit, but does at least demonstrate a simple common domestic practice, spread over several tribal areas.

It must be assumed that the farming economy in the hill country was a mixed one; although mostly pastoral, as it has remained to this present day, some cultivation would have been necessary, yet surprisingly few traces have been noticed. The only suggestion of prehistoric agriculture in the form of Celtic fields has been made on the south end of the Long Mynd by O.G.S. Crawford.[29] There is here a complicated palimpsest of boundary banks and trackways but his observations were based only on a few air photographs. A close study of the situation both from the photographs (fig. 7) and

Fig. 8. Cropmarks of circular enclosures in the Severn Valley near Montford

on the ground shows that these earthworks belong to a long period of time and some of the fields may be as late as the Napoleonic wars.[30] It is clear also from local knowledge of the hills in the surrounding areas that there are very extensive traces of field systems, but they are normally so faint that they would show up only under exceptional circumstances from the air. As one might expect, the hill people were just as active farmers as their contemporaries in the plains and valleys. Intensive field-work will surely change these vague traces into definite patterns.

Perhaps overmuch consideration has been given to the pattern of the distribution of hill-forts, and some account must be taken of the lowland areas which were the most easily cultivated. The light subsoils of the Severn Valley in particular have produced ample evidence, in the form of crop-marks, of early occupation and agriculture. One can only presume that these areas too were parcelled up by the local lords who sent out their warriors at intervals to collect tribute in the form of grain and cattle. There may be strongly defended enclosures in these areas too, but no longer so strikingly visible as the great hill-forts, since they have been eroded by centuries of ploughing (figs. 8, 9). Very few of the

lowland farmsteads have been investigated and our knowledge is entirely due to the work of Mr. W.E. Jenks. This has
been confined to three sites which have appeared as
crop-marks at Weeping Cross, Sharpstones Hill, and Lyth Hill.

Weeping Cross[31] was found to be a large nine-acre (3.5
ha.) site which was excavated under rescue conditions in
advance of housing development, which now covers most of
it. This revealed almost continuous occupation from the
Neolithic period; there were Beaker cremation burials and
several barrows, traces of the Late Bronze Age and so into
the Iron Age and up to the conquest. The pottery shows
Roman influences and the presence of black burnished ware
indicates that occupation extended into the second century.
The Iron Age inhabitants lived in round and sub-rectangular
houses in ditched enclosures, but the finds, reports the
excavator, 'were miserably small and metal almost non-
existent', so that, like those from the hill-forts, they do not
offer evidence of anything more than a poor, backward, rural
community.

Sharpstones Hill, a crop-mark site about ¼ mile south-west
of Weeping Cross, has produced evidence of occupation
similar to that from Weeping Cross — enclosure ditches and
circular huts,[32] one of which, 11 m. in diameter, had been
superseded by a rectangular building (*c.* 13 m. by 5.5 m.).
The circular hut had four posts centrally placed forming a
square (4.5 m.). The pottery from this site indicates continuity into the second century A.D.

Lyth Hill,[33] also a crop-mark site, has Iron Age enclosures
with circular houses, and the finds from the excavations have
been a little more interesting and numerous than those from
the other two sites. They include what is considered to be
early Iron Age pottery, a saddle quern, re-used as a
packing-stone in a post-hole, a clay loom weight, a bronze
eyelet and hundreds of pot-boilers.

These three farmsteads represent cultivation on the sands
and gravels along the south side of the Rea Brook valley and
there are probably many more. The settled occupation is
spread over a long period, but it may be more intermittent
than the present evidence suggests, or possibly people moved
from site to site as conditions became unpleasant with

Fig. 9.   A ditched enclosure at Woolaston, Shrops.

accumulation of domestic rubbish or with soil exhaustion. Nor is it yet clear what happened when the *civitas* became established, although at two of these sites occupation seems to have ceased. This problem, however, must be considered in its proper context below. It is reasonable to assume from the evidence to date, scant though it may be, that there was a considerable scatter of Iron Age farmers exploiting the lighter subsoils in the areas south of the Severn.

This occupation must affect any calculation of population density and Dr. Stanford's figure of 29 per square mile at the time of the Roman conquest is based on the conjectured number of dwellings in the hill-forts only. It is difficult to conceive how, with our very limited amount of information, one could even begin to form the basis of a calculation of the large potential arable areas of Shropshire. One thing is certain; that although only the local lord, his family, retainers and war bands lived in the hill-forts under normal conditions, there were many more people cultivating the land and engaged in a pastoral economy in the hills, or hunting and fishing in the forests, lakes and swamps.

All these fragments of evidence, when brought together, fail to present us with a convincing picture of the peoples who faced the armed might of Rome. The period of greatest strength and unity seems to have ended about 200 B.C. Something then brought about a fragmentation of Celtic society, and what seems to be the pattern by the time of the conquest is a number of local war lords, secure with their band of warriors in their fortress eyries. They probably had territorial claims, doubtless always in dispute, on the crops of the lowland farms, the stock of the hill folk and the hard-won spoils of the hunters and fishers of the forests and swamps. Such a society could not integrate easily in the face of such a powerful opponent, except under a dominant personality, and this is probably why some of the warrior bands fled westwards to join the banner of Caratacus. The Cornovian farmers may even have welcomed the advance of Rome; at least they could look forward to a reasonable system of law, justice and taxation, administered by a civil organisation rather than by the whim of the local tyrant who took what he fancied.

The tribal name and boundaries

The Cornovii may remain to us a faceless people, since they left so little that distinguishes them from any other folk, and the absence of a coinage denies us both an opportunity of estimating their area of influence and knowledge of any names of their rulers. There are, on the other hand, two real pieces of evidence, in their name and in the fact that *Viroconium* was their capital. The name of the capital occurs in several ancient sources. Ptolemy lists it as *Viroconion*, one of the two *poleis* of the tribe (*Geography*, II, 3, 19). It appears three times in the Antonine Itinerary as *Urioconio* (*Iter II*), *Viroconiorum* and *Viriconio* (*Iter XII*),[34] and the Ravenna Cosmography gives *Utriconion Cornoviorum*.[35] No Iron Age community lived on the site, although the land was probably under cultivation and there may have been a few scattered farmsteads. The name was given to the site by the Roman military authority when it was chosen as a base for operations against the peoples to the west. As in many other cases, the name was transferred from a nearby place and the obvious one was the Wrekin whose inhabitants resisted the army. Working from the old Welsh name of the Wrekin, *Cair Guricon*, and the later Anglo-Saxon form, *Wreocen*, Professor Kenneth Jackson has suggested *Uriconon* as a possibility,[36] changed by the Romans, for ease of pronunciation and with a proper Latin ending, to *Viroconium*. With this solution the meaning of the name remains obscure, whereas an alternative, *Viriconon*, could give a meaning 'The Town of Virico'. Virico is a personal name known from Gallic sources[37] and perhaps gives us the name of the last defender of the fortress on the Wrekin. If this should be so, the name of the fortress and city ought to be *Viriconium*, as it appears in *Iter XII*, but in this book the form which has come to find acceptance (*Viroconium*) will be used.

The tribal name is quite certain, thanks to the remarkable inscription found from the collapsed front of the Forum (*RIB* 288), which records the dedication of the building to the Emperor Hadrian by the *CIVITAS CORNOVIORUM* — i.e. the tribe of the Cornovii. The name appears also on a tombstone from Ilkley (*RIB* 634), which depicts a lady, said to be thirty years old, her hair in two long plaits (fig. 10) and described in the inscription as –*C(IVIS) CORNOVIA*. The formula on the stone indicates an early date, probably the end of the first century, and the woman must be considered as a camp follower. But the presence of the relief shows that someone with Romanised ideas cared sufficiently to pay for this expensive monument, and provides the nearest approach one can get at present to a real native.

The tribal name also appears in the *Notitia Dignitatum* (*Occ.*, XL 34) as a later army unit, *Coh. Prima Cornoviorum Ponte Aeli*, stationed at Newcastle-upon-Tyne. The Ravenna Cosmography preserves the name in its entry *UTRICONION CORNOVIORUM*[38] and Ptolemy lists the tribe as *Cornavioi*. There are two other tribes of this name, one given by Ptolemy in north-west Scotland (*Geography* II, 3 19) and the other in a place name in the Ravenna Cosmography west of the Tamar in Cornwall. The name is given as *PURO-CORONAVIS* (No. 6), clearly a scribal error for *DURO-CORNAVIS*, which means 'the fortress of the Cornovii', and it is this tribe which has given its name to the peninsula – Cornwall. Thus there are three tribes in Britain widely separated having the same name, and it has been considered by most scholars to be the Roman way of denoting 'the people of the peninsula', from the Latin word *cornu*. This could well apply to the tribe living in the tip of Cornwall, providing the geography was evident, as it might have been to Roman surveyors establishing military sites and communications in the first century.

This particular meaning hardly applies, however, to Shropshire and Caithness. Another possibility has been urged by Anne Ross in the primary use of the word *cornu* to mean 'a horn'. As she has indicated, horned deities, with their obvious symbolism, were very important in Celtic religion.[39] Although there is no direct connection with any of the Cornovii tribes, it is interesting to reflect on the strange survival of the famous Abbots Bromley horn dance derived from pagan ritual. Abbots Bromley lies only 55 km. east-north-east of Wroxeter in a direct line. Professor Charles Thomas has made a good case for regarding some of the tribal names in Scotland as deriving from cult and totemic animals and birds

Fig 10. A tombstone, from Ilkley, of Vedica, a Cornovian (*RIB* 634)

like the horse, sheep, raven and boar[40] and this may well apply to the Cornovii of the Shropshire Plain.

A much more difficult problem is the area of the tribe. It will be appreciated by those who have read the other volumes of this series that the tribal areas, as we now understand them, were devised to suit the Roman arrangements for dividing Britain into suitable self-governing territories, and may or may not relate to the original boundaries of the tribes. Many small or insignificant tribes disappeared; for example, Caesar lists four tribes in south-eastern Britain of whom there is no subsequent trace.[41] Nor are the lists of the *civitates* complete and new epigraphic discoveries make additions. For example an inscription from Brougham (Cumb.) has introduced the Carvetii[42] and a *graffito* on a tile found at Caves Inn, near Rugby, refers to a *civitas Corielsoliliorum.*[43] As seen above (p. 7) the probable area of the original tribe extended well beyond the modern county of Shropshire towards the west and north, but the boundaries on the other two sides may have been much the same. When one attempts to connect this area with the known neighbouring tribes, the Brigantes to the north, the Coritani to the east, and the Dobunni to the south, it is difficult to do so without extending the tribal territory much further into Cheshire, Staffordshire, Hereford and Worcestershire. While this is by no means impossible, one cannot but wonder if there could not have been other *civitates* to occupy those vast spaces. Tribal capitals are normally recognised by their regular grid street plan and public buildings, such as are found at Wroxeter, Leicester and Cirencester. The other towns, such as Wall, which may be considered likely candidates as the centres for any missing tribes, have none of these characteristics. Either, then, we accept the large territory, or our understanding of the Roman local government system is inadequate.

Other important factors are connected with the military occupation of adjacent areas. Very little is known about the relationship between *civitates* in frontier areas and the army.[44] The amount of freedom allowed to a tribe would depend on individual circumstances. It might be possible for garrisons to be permanently stationed within the tribal area, providing they were performing a limited function, such as the protection of a main road, or a river crossing. Thus one could visualise the small unit at Wall, maintaining a watch on the principal route from the south to the military areas of north Wales and the north-west. But this could still be within the domain of the tribe. The troops would be under the military law and have full control over their *territorium*, which was probably a small area around the fort, providing the unit with the necessary tactical areas required for defence and grazing for their animals.[45] There was a well-established code governing the behaviour of troops in civil areas which gave rise to many disputes and legal action.[46] Constant trouble is recorded over supplies and their just payments.[47]

Where there was a net-work of forts controlling the whole of an area and its population, one might expect complete military government. As the army moved forward or withdrew in conquest and consolidation, the situation must have changed. The only historical account of events of this nature comes from Tacitus[48] and concerns the Frisii between the Elbe and the Weser. This tribe gave Corbulo hostages and the general marked out their *territorium* and gave them a senate, magistrates and laws. To see that this arrangement was maintained, he established a fort in the area. This is a clear example of the creation of a *civitas* in a newly conquered area in which there were garrisoned troops. The arrangement did not last very long, since Claudius soon withdrew all his troops to the Rhine. A similar sequence of events may account for the creation of the *civitas Carvetii* behind the western end of Hadrian's Wall in the third century. In the long period of peace many of the garrisons were withdrawn and their forts dismantled and the creation of a civil area of self-government became possible.[49]

It seems reasonable to suppose that the Cornovii remained wholly under military control until *c.* 90 when *Legio XX* finally gave up its fortress at Wroxeter. This could have been the occasion for the creation of the *civitas.* The boundary of the tribe must have marched with that of the military zone to the west and the south. The first permanent fort westwards is Forden Gaer on the Severn and one must, therefore, seek the boundary to the east; this possibly is approximately to the line of Offa's Dyke. The nearest known forts to the south are the Leintwardine complex[50] and at Wall Town[51] in the Clee Hills. There is a fort north of Craven Arms, but the date remains unknown. The Clees could have remained in army control and the tribal lands may not have extended much beyond Bridgnorth to the south. To the west lies Wall, halfway between Wroxeter and Leicester, and the boundary may have been hereabouts. Much of Staffordshire could have been included up to the fort at Newcastle-under-Lyme,[52] but it is not yet certain when this was abandoned. To the north lay the *territorium* of the Chester Legion, and although Ptolemy placed Deva in the *civitas*, it surely must be excluded while the legion was there, and the problem is to estimate how large the *territorium* was and how far it extended to the south. Apart from the space immediately around the fortress needed for the harbour, store-compounds and cemeteries, there were at Chester stone quarries and the portage station at Heronbridge.[53] Lands were also required for grazing and tilling. In a case from the Rhineland quoted by Tacitus[54] the Frisii occupied lands which were left vacant but kept for army use along the bank of the Rhine. When they were ordered out, they sent a petition to Nero, who rejected their request to remain there. The order was later enforced by a unit of auxiliary cavalry, but another tribe, the Ampsivarii, then settled in the same lands. Their advocate, Boiocalus, in an impassioned speech, asked why such an area of vacant ground should lie waste merely on the assumption that some time in the distant future the flocks and herds of the troops could be brought into graze. In the end, this tribe was also driven out by force of arms. It is not clear whether in this case the lands belonged to a legionary *territorium* or represented an *ager publicus populi Romani*. But it does seem clear from this example that the army did make claim to extensive domains for their exclusive use in tilling and grazing. If the Chester area extended down the Dee as far as Holt, it could have included the legionary works depot, and presumably full control of the river was needed for shipment of the heavy loads to Heronbridge. A conclusion could be reached that the tribal boundary may be about halfway between Whitchurch and Chester.[55] This still leaves the problem of east Cheshire. Northwich and Middlewich were important in Roman times for the salt-works and it is not unlikely that they were under the control of a *procurator*. This may be also the situation to the north-east, where in the Peak District of Derbyshire the stamps on lead pigs gave us the name of the district *Lutudarum*, and where forts at Rocester and Littlechester indicate army occupation into the late second century.

The possibilities considered above may be true of the first two centuries of Roman rule in Britain, but changes were gradually taking place. This is no place to discuss the pressures on the Roman Empire or their effects; they were too large and too complicated. One result, however, was to divide provinces into smaller units of administration. Thus, during the Severan period, Britain became two provinces. There was also a gradual merging of civil and military functions. The army had grown in numbers and its presence was felt more and more in civil administration. The boundaries so carefully established between the self-governing tribes and the military zones ceased to be meaningful.

In these circumstances, it seems most likely that when an area ceased to be fully occupied by the army, instead of adding the territory to an existing *civitas*, a new one would be created, as in the case of the Carvetii.[56] Any new tribal capital thus created would not have the features of those established in the earlier centuries. The square street grid and public buildings would no longer be considered necessary. Without epigraphic evidence it would, therefore, be difficult to identify any possible new capital. Prosperity and expansion are common to most of the towns of Roman Britain in the later period. The *graffito* on a roof tile found at Caves Inn, near Rugby, giving the name of a *civitas* which is otherwise unknown, could have come into being through the reorganisation of government and administration in the third century.[57]

2.

History: A. D. 43 - 367

The thick fog of ignorance which at present surrounds the pre-Roman period lifts dramatically with the Roman conquest, but not immediately. In the initial phase of A.D. 43-8 the Roman army was engaged in consolidating its gains south and east of the Trent and the lower Severn. Anxious to gain acceptance in the areas beyond, it is possible that a king of the Cornovii was among the eleven who submitted to Claudius,[1] but it was not until the second governor, Ostorius Scapula, arrived in Britain that the full impact of Rome was felt in the middle Severn.

The Belgic prince Caratacus, realising that he could not hold the Roman army in the south-east, had established himself as leader of the tribes inhabitating what is now Wales and roused them against Rome. He carried out a well-timed attack deep into Roman-held territory, presumably Gloucestershire. Scapula stabilised the situation but soon saw that it was impossible to deal with these hostile activities from the frontier established by Plautius between the Humber and the lower Severn, so he moved the army westwards towards the Severn to search out and bring Caratacus to bay. To do this it was necessary to take troops from the south-east from areas not yet wholly pacified; the legion in reserve, the XXth at Colchester, was moved, probably to the Kingsholm site at Gloucester, to protect the vital crossing of the lower Severn. In its place a *colonia* or settlement of retired veterans was established. These old soldiers could act as a reserve force deep in the rear and at the same time give the Britons a demonstration of urban life and model citizenship. In the latter they singularly failed, since their rough behaviour and contempt for the local inhabitants soon roused deep feelings which were later to take positive shape in the holocaust of A.D. 60.

Scapula planned the campaigns with a sense of urgency and purpose and with strategical insight, although the brief account of Tacitus[2] as usual telescopes the events of several years into a few sentences. The fact that Caratacus moved his base of operations from south to central Wales would seem to indicate that Scapula planned at first to encircle him in Silurian territory. Once the target shifted to central Wales the site of Wroxeter comes into immediate significance, since it is the obvious site for a base for any campaign into the heart of Wales. Caratacus had chosen his site well in his attempt to block the Roman advance into the heartland of Wales; the wooded and hilly terrain was very difficult for the legionaries and impossible for cavalry. The legions were forced to make a frontal assault up a steep slope and although the battle was won by the Romans, the British tribesmen melted away into the woods. Scapula was now in a difficult position, and had Caratacus persuaded Cartimandua, the client queen of the Brigantes, to throw in her lot with him, it could have been desperate for the Romans. The wily queen remained loyal to Rome and Caratacus was trapped and handed over in chains to grace the triumph of Claudius.

Scapula had no brief to go forward to conquer and occupy Wales; his instructions were to deal with Caratacus and no more, so he had to maintain a frontier in wild wooded country, with the Silures now fighting for their very existence in persistent and effective guerrilla warfare. It is not difficult to read between the terse lines of Tacitus to appreciate the serious losses the army was now suffering in the field. Scapula died in 51/52 from an illness intensified by sheer exhaustion, frustration and failure. Although his successor, Didius Gallus, stabilised the situation it remained grim enough and it may have been at this time that there was talk in Rome of giving up Britain altogether. Seneca, who as advisor to the young Nero would have been fully conversant with the situation, began to call in the loans to British chiefs, an action which contributed to the growth of anti-Roman sentiment.[3]

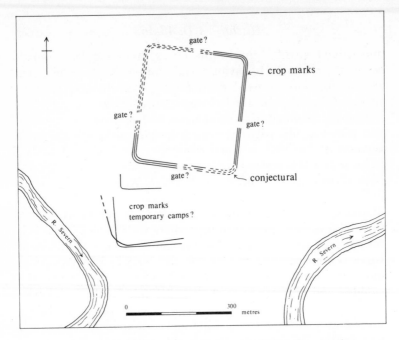

Fig. 11. The military fort and camps at Eaton Constantine

Through this period of fierce border warfare the military base at Wroxeter must have seen the build-up of summer forces and their dispersal to winter quarters every year. There is growing archaeological evidence of the presence of forts and marching camps.[4] Some of these are near the site of the later Roman city, but there is another group, identified from the air by Mr. Arnold Baker, 5 km. to the south-east near Eaton Constantine (fig. 11). One of these forts is about twenty acres (8 ha.) in size and may be a legionary base.[5] None of these early military sites has yet been dated, but their relationship to the Wrekin would imply that these military activities were directed at the hill-fort on this famous peak and there is recent archaeological evidence of its final destruction by fire (above, p.10). To these sites must be added that of the auxiliary fort by the River Severn, south of Wroxeter, which from an aerial photograph (fig. 12) would appear to have been a permanent fort.[6]

The most important sequence of military sites was along the supply route from the south-east, and this great Roman

Fig. 12. An auxiliary fort on the Severn south of Wroxeter

arterial road linking London with the north-west, known later as Watling Street, remained throughout all ages as one of the key military roads in Britain, its significance being reinforced when it became the vital link between London and Ireland, seen as Telford's great Holyhead Road. The advance post established by Plautius was beyond the Fosse Way at *Manduessedum* (Mancetter)[7] and the first Scapulan site along this route was at Wall, where a sandstone ridge provided a dominant site facing the north-west. At this stage it was possible that *Legio XIV* was established here, a position commanding the Midland Gap, the supply route, and well placed to support the forward campaigns. Excavations have recovered fragments of a very large Claudian military base, but its defences and function have yet to be defined.[8] *Pennocrucium*, the next site along the road, has produced (as crop-marks) a number of forts and marching camps[9] clearly indicating its military importance at the junction of the main routes to Wroxeter and Chester, but as yet little investigation has been done on any of them. The next site is the vantage point on the high ground at Red Hill, overlooking the plain to the west. This was obviously occupied by a fort or signal station, but the crop-marks recorded are difficult to interpret, recent excavations have not been helpful, and the site is now largely destroyed by a reservoir.[10] Between these sites are two marching camps near Watling Street at Burlington[11] which must be associated with this early period.

There is little trace, so far, of any other early camp or forts along the frontier to the south, apart from marching camps at Bromfield[12] and a 3¾ acre fort at Stretford Bridge near Craven Arms,[13] which are difficult to see in any later context. A line of strategical importance, which one might reasonably assume the Romans would have wished to control, is that of the later Roman road south-west from Wroxeter. This goes through the Church Stretton gap via Leintwardine, where there is a succession of forts from the Neronian-Flavian period,[14] into the Herefordshire plain to cross the Wye near Kenchester. It is clear from recent discoveries at Usk[15] that Scapula held the Usk Valley, so there must have been a route from Abergavenny to Kenchester.

The reconnaissance raid of Scapula early in his campaign against the Decangi (or Cenngi), who are presumably the Deceangli of Flintshire (above p. 8), provoked a reaction from Brigantia and this may have prevented him from sealing off contact between north Wales and Cheshire, allowing Caratacus to escape this way. It is likely, however, that Whitchurch would have been held and part of the Severn Valley beyond Wroxeter, but evidence for all these possibilities is at present lacking.

Summing up the situation at this time, the greater part of the territory of the Cornovii was held by the army (fig. 13), and this would have given little opportunity for the tribe to have displayed any hostility to Rome. Contact with the soldiers brought a new dimension into the lives of these people. The sudden impact of a new, splendid civilisation may have been overwhelming and fearsome, but soon they began to appreciate that bargains could be made, that they had things to trade. The army needed food, especially fresh vegetables, eggs, poultry, game, honey, cheese and milk and more powerful drinks, and of equal urgency they needed women. In the wake of the army there were traders and the middlemen who would set out immediately to organise local goods and services for the troops. Quite soon communities would appear and hastily constructed shanty towns outside the forts and fortresses. Under strict military control the natives would soon learn to come to terms with the conquerors and that it could also be profitable. All the later settlements in the area would have originated in this way and the largest and most important would have been that of Wroxeter.

The policy of a limited conquest, initiated by Claudius, led to the difficulties the Roman army had in establishing a satisfactory frontier beyond the Severn.[16] The problem was resolved by the young Nero who, in the early days of his reign, was guided by his two elderly counsellors, Seneca and Burrus. It may have been they who advised on a total or partial withdrawal, since a much better frontier line could have been based on the Severn. But Nero saw a chance of military glory, a completion of the work of his distinguished ancestors Caesar and Claudius, and so decided on the total conquest of Wales. It is worthy of note that at the same time the great general Corbulo was sent to Armenia to deal with the problems of the Parthian frontier. A bright young military man, Quintus Veranius, was selected[17] and sent to Britain in the winter 57-8, and although he died after his first season, his campaign must have been of some effect against the Silures as the tribe appears to give no further trouble. Veranius was immediately succeeded by another experienced general, C. Suetonius Paullinus, who concentrated on central

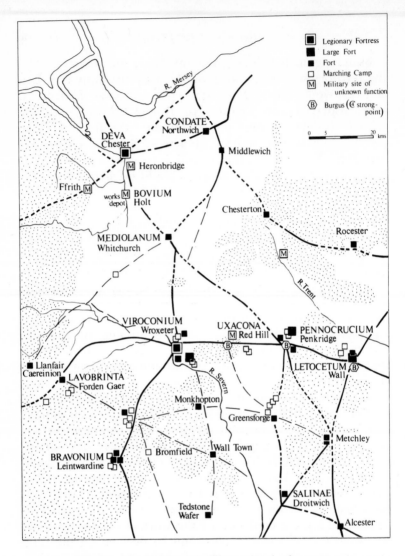

Fig. 13. Distribution of military sites in the canton

Wales and Snowdonia. By now the Romans had come to appreciate the wide-spread and powerful influence of the Druids. This priestly hierarchy had fled from their sacred groves near the British capital, *Camulodunum*, and taken refuge in the remote but fertile land of Anglesey. These priests with their close connections to the British ruling houses were to maintain and foster the anti-Roman feelings.

Fig. 14. A bronze handle (15 cm. long) in the form of an eagle's head, probably from the legionary occupation, found at Wroxeter

Resistance to Roman rule in the rest of Britain could be crushed by the destruction of the Druids and their religious centre. Thus Anglesey became the main target of the Roman thrust towards the north-west.

The story of subsequent events, with the great British rising led by Boudicca in 60, have little place in this survey of the Cornovii and have been dealt with fully elsewhere.[18] It is extremely doubtful if the tribe was in any position to take part, except through a few dissentients, in this tragic story, and their territory was now firmly under army control. As the front had moved forward, Wroxeter had assumed a more important role. The great strategic value of the site as a campaign base had been fully recognised. It had been permanently held by an auxiliary unit in its fort on the river south of Wroxeter. This was perhaps a *cohors equitata* of Thracians, since a tombstone of a trooper of this unit was found in 1725.[19] With the decision to move forward and conquer and occupy the whole of Wales came the establishment at Wroxeter of the legionary fortress of the XIVth legion, probably moved forward from Wall (fig. 14). The presence of *Legio XIV* at Wroxeter was known long ago from the discovery of tombstones of soldiers of this legion in the cemetery north-east of the city when the ground was being brought under cultivation in the eighteenth century. The soldiers thus commemorated are Titus Flaminius,[20] depicted in relief above the inscription (though only his boots survive) and Marcus Petronius,[21] a standard-bearer. A fragment of another military tombstone gives part of the number XII [II], almost certainly the XIVth.[22] There is a stone of Gaius Mannius Secundus of *Legio XX*,[23] but he was a *beneficiarius* on the governor's staff where he would have administrative duties which could have taken him anywhere in the province.

For many years the site of the legionary fortress was not known, although the light sandy subsoil at Wroxeter is particularly suitable for crop-marks and these were studied from the air year by year. It was not until the 1950s that J.K. St. Joseph observed and recorded two ditches forming a carefully set-out corner in the north-west area of the Roman city,[24] and evidently predating the civil buildings and streets. Proof was not, however, forthcoming until part of the area surrounding the *piscina* of the bath-house was excavated as part of the programme of a training school. A sequence of timber buildings of first-century date was found, on the same alignment as the ditches (figs. 15, 16). It then became evident that the fortress of the XIVth lay buried deep below the Roman city and this is why it had never produced crop-marks. The excavations also showed that there were several periods of building which must reflect the movement of the legions. The Wroxeter fortress would have been part of a system of permanent establishments planted in the territory of the Cornovii to control movement of hostile gatherings and keep an eye on the tribe as a whole. To the north, the obvious site for a fort is Whitchurch on the site of the Roman town of *Mediolanum*. The only excavations carried out there were those of 1962 by Professor Barri Jones on a rather limited area.[25] Nevertheless contact was made with timber buildings of a military character of the Flavian period associated with a ditch and rampart. There was a suggestion of earlier occupation which may indicate that the military occupation began when *Legio XIV* built its fortress at Wroxeter; an important establishment of this kind would not have been left in a totally exposed position.

The great revolt of Boudicca had brought further conquests to a halt. The army pursued a campaign of vengeance which became almost a vendetta in the hands of Paullinus. He was recalled and more conciliatory governors sent to Britain.

Fig. 15. The construction slots of the legionary buildings and pits in the clean sand below the bath-house levels

The revolt had forced the Roman government to a new policy towards Britain which involved the people in a greater degree of Romanisation and urban development. Apart from the *colonia* at *Camulodunum* and the possible *municipium* of *Verulamium* there appears to have been little development along this line before 60, although the province was doubtless flooded with mass-produced merchandise, pottery, glass and metal ware.

So Britain gradually recovered from the revolt and its aftermath. Governors were chosen for their administrative abilities and receive brief, almost contemptuous, comments from Tacitus; but Petronius Turpilianus and Trebellius Maximus pursued this new policy successfully. By A.D. 66 Nero thought it safe to detach *Legio XIV*, made famous for its great victory over Boudicca, for an ambitious project in the East. This involved a reorganisation of the British legions and the Wroxeter fortress was now occupied by the XXth from Gloucester, where its place there was taken by *Legio II Augusta.* Excavations below the modern, mediaeval and Roman cities of Gloucester have revealed some of the new timber barracks securely dated by coins to this period.[26] It would seem that the site of the fortress was moved from Kingsholm, where timber buildings of the early site have been found, to somewhat higher ground. At Wroxeter the same site appears to have been kept in commission. But the area so far explored is far too small to be sure of this and one is tempted to link structural changes with historical events. At the same time it is likely that *Legio IX* was moved to Lincoln. It appears formally to have been split into at least two forces, one at Longthorpe on the Nene, near Peterborough and the other elsewhere.

The Empire was riven by the Civil War of 69 which brought the Flavian dynasty to the throne, but the tragedies on the Rhine, parts of Gaul and northern Italy did not spread to Britain. The cause of Vespasian must have been strong in Britain and it is possible that his son Titus may have served here as a military tribune.[27] Cogidubnus had been the main instrument of the new emperor in his conquest of the south-west in A.D. 43 and the British king could now have supported his old colleague with the British notables and

Fig. 16. The section in the main *praefurnium* showing the three main
deposits: (*A*) the military, (*B*) bathhouse construction, (*C*)
praefurnium dump

possibly even with the legionary commanders. It is an
interesting speculation that the title he received, *legatus
augusti*, may have been an honoured award given by
Vespasian during his reign.[28]

The peaceful situation in Britain was soon to be changed
by Venutius, the consort of Queen Cartimandua, for trouble
had long been brewing between this pair, linked by a dynastic
marriage. The disturbances of A.D. 69 gave Venutius a
chance to assert himself, take over Brigantia and to declare
his hostility to Rome. This was a problem which had to be
resolved as soon as the revolt of Civilis was crushed, and in
A.D. 71 Vespasian sent one of his most distinguished
generals, Petillius Cerialis, as Governor to Britain. Not only
had he special knowledge of Britain from his service here as
legate of *Legio IX* in A.D. 60, but as a son-in-law of the
Emperor he could be trusted.

The military task in subduing Brigantia required additional
legionary strength and he brought with him the *Legio II*

Adiutrix, a legion raised during the Civil War and as yet untried. It was obvious that Cerialis would take his old legion, the IXth, for his spearhead in his advance to the north and the new legion took over the Lincoln fortress as a reserve force. The XXth, now commanded by Agricola, also took part[29] but its role in this short but decisive campaign remains uncertain.

Venutius, it is presumed, chose Stanwick[30] as the place to face the Romans, but he failed like so many before and after, and Brigantia was conquered. Next it was the turn of Wales for total subjugation and this was the task of Julius Frontinus with the help of *II Augusta* and *XX Valeria Victrix*. This involved the establishment of *II Augusta* in a new fortress at Caerleon on the Usk, but the XXth was well placed at Wroxeter to deal with North Wales and to keep watch on the western part of Brigantia.

The situation changed once more with the coming of Cnaeus Julius Agricola as Governor and the decision to extend the conquest of the north. Agricola used the IXth and XXth, the former now established in the Vale of York, possibly at York itself, and doubtless detachments from the other two, but he intended the main battle honours to go to his old command, the XXth. The first seasons involved the legion in activities in Brigantia and southern Scotland. As the bases were established, there must have been provision for a legionary headquarters in the north, but at a rearward position. An ideal place would have been Carlisle and if this was the intention, its place on the west could have been taken by *II Adiutrix*, now no longer needed in reserve at Lincoln. The circumstances of Wales and Brigantia had also changed and Wroxeter was no longer the best site. A more obvious one was Chester, on the Dee estuary, with a direct contact with the Irish Sea, now so necessary for the northern campaign. So, at some stage in the progress of Agricola, Chester became the legionary base for *Legio II Adiutrix*, which had the advantage of allowing the XXth to retain Wroxeter until the full complement of the legion could be transferred to the north. With the decision to advance beyond the Forth in A.D. 83 and the decisive defeat of the Caledonian tribes there was a need for a base even further to the north, now that Scotland was to be held, so the great fortress at Inchtuthil on the Tay was established.[31] The excavations of Sir Ian Richmond and Professor J.K.S. St. Joseph recovered the plan of its timber buildings and dated the occupation at least down to A.D. 86. The construction work must have been started some years earlier in A.D. 84 or 85, but it was never completed; the *praetorium* or commandant's house, at least two tribunes' houses, a granary and other buildings are missing. The work had reached this stage when the imperial decision was made to withdraw from the territory north of the Forth-Clyde line, so the legionaries promptly stopped building and began to dismantle everything.

This is not the place to consider the reasons behind this change of policy, forced on Domitian by the events on the Danube where the Romans had suffered serious defeats in A.D. 86-7. Troops were urgently needed to exact revenge and restore the balance of power. Doubts may already have been voiced about the advisability of holding Scotland with little hope of economic return. Britain reverted to a three-legion establishment and it was *Legio II Adiutrix* which had to leave, making it logical for the XXth to move south, not to its old base at Wroxeter, but to the new one at Chester. As soon as this decision was made, headquarters staff packed up their records and made, no doubt thankfully, the short journey to Chester, instead of the dreaded trek to the distant wilds. Presently the demolition gangs moved in and took down the timber buildings, filled in all the trenches, holes and ditches, buried the debris and left a clean levelled site. When today one excavates at Wroxeter at about six feet from present ground level, a very distinctive layer is reached. It is about a foot thick, grey-purple in colour flecked with red and black, so universal and outstanding that students christened it 'the plum pudding layer', which sobriquet has remained. It is the levelled and trampled debris of the demolished fortress, compounded of tiny fragments of the daub filling from the walls and securely dated by a coin of A.D. 86.[32] Below it are the pits, tanks, latrines and construction slots which form the substructures of successive occupations and buildings (fig. 17). One of the pits, the latest of the series, produced many

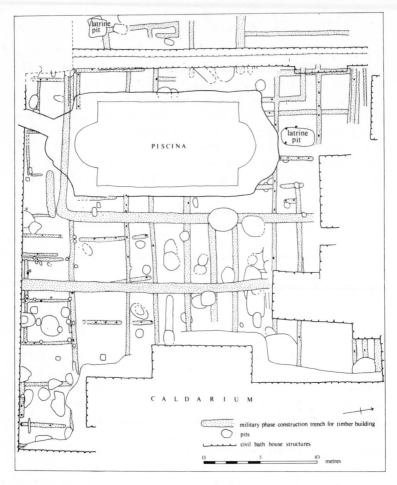

Fig. 17. The legionary remains beneath the baths at Wroxeter

fragments of twisted and distorted pottery. When the quartermaster came to clear the store, he found these vessels which no soldier would have accepted as replacements. Now all these seconds and thirds, which some wily potter had packed in the bottom of a crate and which had therefore missed inspection, were thrown out and shovelled into a convenient hole. An establishment move is always a good time for writing off old and unwanted stock and preparing fresh lists.

When the last soldiers departed from *Viroconium* they would have left more than a bare plateau, for somewhere beyond the fortress defences were *canabae* and a civil settlement. The difference between the two is that the former were entirely under military control and all traders and shop-keepers held short-lease tenancies renewable every five years; this enabled the army to exercise authority over sale of goods and hygiene. As soon as soldiers retired and wished to settle down near their old comrades still in arms, they would not wish to remain under such control and found accommodation outside the military limits, and in this way there would gradually develop an independant civil community with its own self-government on the pattern of a *vicus.* *Canabae* are usually to be found near the fortress and the civil settlement at a distance, as at York, where the latter is on the other side of the river.[33] One cannot recognise two separate areas of civil occupation at *Viroconium* but an obvious place for one is by the river harbour, where the docks and warehouses could have been built and the army would need to keep control of the river crossing. It is possible that *canabae* were allowed to develop on either or both sides of the fortress to the north and south outside the main gates. This would help to explain the odd street plan north of the central *insulae* of the city,[34] but there could have been another centre between the fortress and the river stretching down to the harbour. Any subsequent civil settlement would have been beyond these limits and presumably to the south, where much of the present village of Wroxeter now stands, but to date very little archaeological trace of these early sites has been noted. A trench cut in 1972 to locate the main road between fortress and river produced evidence of glass working at this period, and a small works here to supply the needs of the troops and civilians is not surprising.[35]

The presence of some six thousand well-paid men would have attracted many of the local natives to the site, drawn there by the lucrative idea of supplying services and food for real cash, a new economic concept. All troops need to supplement their adequate but unexciting military diet; above all they are permanently thirsty. *Tabernae* would automatically spring into being and, of course, brothels for all tastes and pockets; a market would appear, and traders selling goods from distant places. But not all the legionaries

were satisfied with easy prostitution, most of them wanted a
more settled way of life with homes and families. Although
they were not allowed to make a legal contract, stable family
life was normal and could be ratified on discharge; children
born *in castris* were common enough all over the Empire.
When legionaries were discharged after their 20 years service
it was natural for them to settle down near their old
companions, but outside the *canabae*. Thus the community
gradually expanded with each discharge and this in its turn
generated more trade. Many of the natives would have come
to live in the town as labourers and servants and sell their
produce of vegetables, fruit, honey etc., in the market. The
population of *canabae* and civil settlement could have been at
least eight to ten thousand people by the time the legion was
due to move to Chester.

In permanent legionary establishments throughout the
Empire these civil settlements grew into large cities and many
received municipal honours,[36] but the problem here is what
happened to all these people when the legion was moved. The
more active and those whose livelihood depended on the
troops went north with the legion, and eventually to Chester,
but inertia must have left more than a remnant. The prospect
of moving permanently into the untamed north in 84 would
not have been attractive to all, and the situation is complicated by the moving of *Legio II Adiutrix* from Lincoln to
Chester *c*. A.D. 78. Traders, and others with no particular
loyalty[37] or affiliation to *Legio XX*, would have gone to
Chester and attached themselves to the new fortress.

In three examples in Britain of legionary fortresses being
given up (at Colchester, Lincoln and Gloucester) the sites
became settlements for army veterans (*coloniae*). Wroxeter is
the exception, although its future must have been decided at
the same time as those of Lincoln and Gloucester.[38] Two
new *coloniae* were considered adequate for army needs and
Wroxeter became the site for the new tribal capital of the
Cornovii.

The second and third centuries

The history of the city is considered in some detail in the

next chapter since it cannot be easily separated from the study of particular buildings. The army began to dismantle all their structures in A.D. 86 and by A.D. 90, the whole area was presumably bare; the only surviving elements of this great fortress may have been some of the main streets needed up to the last moment for carting away the re-usable timbers and loads of rubbish which could not be buried. Communication had also to be maintained between the *canabae*, the civil settlement and the routes to the north of the fortress, and if one of these crossed the military area it would have to be preserved. The planning of the city was probably carried out by military engineers and it is even possible that a working party stayed on to construct the main streets and their drainage systems. It was also the opinion of Professor Donald Atkinson that the early city bath-house was military work,[39] so similar was the masonry to that of the buildings in the fortress at Chester. There must have been skilled masons in the army there, since there was at least one building of stone in what was otherwise a completely timber fortress; this was the bath-house. The massive building along the *via praetoria* at Chester is primary; there are no earlier timber buildings and it must, therefore, belong to the Agricolan foundation *c.* 78.[40] An earlier bath-house has been found at Exeter which can only be associated with the presence of *Legio II Augusta* between A.D. 50 and 66.[41] On this evidence one might reasonably assume that a legionary bath-house exists somewhere within the fortress at *Viroconium*, but there is no hint of it in any aerial photographs. It would also suggest that there was a body of soldier masons at Wroxeter capable of erecting such a complicated building. If Atkinson's hypothesis is correct, the fact that the work was never completed may be readily explained, since the sudden cessation could have been brought about by an emergency situation demanding troops elsewhere. There is precisely such a situation in *c.* A.D. 100 with the rising of the tribes of Scotland and the destruction of the northern forts. This trail of disaster can be traced as far south as Corbridge where it has been thought to be dated by a coin hoard, the latest item of which is A.D. 98.[42] The most dramatic evidence has come from Newstead, when the excavations early in the century produced a magnificent haul of military equipment,[43] which came from pits dug by the army detachments sent later to recover the Roman dead and tidy up the site. The date of this event has been given by Sir Ian Richmond, following the further work at Newstead, as 'not much beyond A.D. 100 on existing evidence',[44] and this has been confirmed by Mr. Brian Hartley in his detailed study of the samian.[45] It is quite evident that between A.D. 95 and A.D. 105 a very serious situation arose in the north. More than ten years had passed since the Caledonian tribes had been so thoroughly beaten by Agricola and they must have observed with surprise the withdrawal south of the Clyde-Forth line. Not understanding the reasons for it, they saw it as a sign of Roman weakness, and by *c.* A.D. 100 they were strong enough to exact sudden vengeance, which must have taken the Romans completely by surprise. It was a state of emergency in which troops were needed immediately in the north to seal off the frontier and carry out reprisal action. Yet it was soon over, since the legions were back at their depots by A.D. 107, rebuilding their defences in stone.[46] One might draw a further conclusion, that if the army were responsible for the erection of the bath-house at *Viroconium*, masons would have been unable to return to complete the work after the actions in the north, since they were now fully occupied at Chester in the large rebuilding programme, presumably delayed by the disaster in the north.

This is all very speculative, but there is one piece of evidence which may have a bearing on the problem. In the *palaestra* of the baths, a stone-lined well was found,[47] and in the filling were tiles and a piece of architectural moulding definitely linking it with the construction of the bath-house. The filling also produced a military camp kettle and a pioneer's axe, demonstrating that legionaries were present at the time, since such bulky objects were not likely to be lying around after the demolition party had cleared the site. These objects belong to an operation subsequent to the demolition of the fortress and the only problem is the time interval which elapsed between clearance and construction. It is difficult to estimate just how much work had been done at the moment when it all stopped. One of the rooms of a

Fig. 18. An inscription to Hadrian from the forum at Wroxter

laconicum suite had not been excavated for the insertion of the underfloor heating system, but there are cornice mouldings, which suggest that in some parts the walls had reached roof height. Even so, it is doubtful if more than two or three seasons' construction had been carried out, which implies a gap of several years between the two operations. Unfortunately, the date of the construction could not be firmly established by the excavation; although five coins were found, including two of Domitian, it is not clear from the report exactly which they are of those listed.[48]

After the unfortunate start of the new city, the central area remained desolate for twenty years; either the community did not want to move or it may have been due to bureaucratic inertia. Eventually, *c.* A.D. 125, perhaps coincidental with the visit to Britain of the Emperor Hadrian (who may have visited *Viroconium* in A.D. 122 on his way north to organise the frontier), things began to move again. The sites were cleared and a rebuilding programme put in hand with the dedication of the forum, in A.D. 130, (fig. 18) on the site of the unfinished bath-house. It is from this time that the city grew and developed. The completion of the forum must have provided the impetus for a general movement into the new city, although evidence is at present sadly lacking. The next event was the fire of *c.* A.D. 160, which swept away the timber shops found by Bushe-Fox and badly damaged the forum. The shops in the front portico facing the street were destroyed; samian vessels were found still in their stacks on the floor, and in another place about a hundred stone bars were discovered, rough-cuts for whetstones, which must have been in a crate. Many of the samian pots were still in the nests in which they had been stacked,

but all lying on their sides, suggesting that they had slid off a
shelf into the silt of the portico gutter. The latest coin
associated with this destruction is one of Pius (A.D. 155),
and a close study of the samian, which includes seventy-three
potters' stamps, indicates a date not very long after A.D. 155
and probably in the decade A.D. 155-65. There is nothing to
suggest that this was any more than an accidental town fire,
in all probability exacerbated by a strong wind, and the
numerous wooden buildings, together with a totally inadequate fire service. Though the main walls of the forum
survived, the rebuilding of it must have been extensive, with
replacement of timber work, including the roof trusses.

The city began to flourish in the second half of the second
century, but until much more excavation is carried out it will
be impossible to illustrate this in detail. There is, however,
important evidence which suggests the size of the city at this
time. There are indications, first noticed by Miss Kenyon,[49]
of defences on the north side of the city but south of the Bell
Brook. There was a prominent bank in the north-east sector
until it was reduced, to facilitate ploughing a few years ago,
to a slight swelling in the ground. This line has been studied
on the west side by Mr. Arnold Baker, who has shown that it
can be postulated for the whole of the north side too and
also that there is a street (or bank?) on the inside of it.[50]
These defences have not yet been excavated so their date is
not known and it is possible they belong to *canabae*
established on the north side of the legionary fortress, rather
than an early city defensive system. Like most of the other
cities and towns of Roman Britain, *Viroconium* was provided
with defences at the end of the second century. This is
generally agreed to have been the work of Clodius Albinus,
then governor of Britain, as part of a scheme to put the
province into a state of readiness for barbarian attacks when
he withdrew most of the army to challenge Severus for the
purple in Gaul in A.D. 196.[51] These defences consisted of a
large bank, two or three ditches and presumably timber gates
and a palisaded walk. The area enclosed was probably about
200 acres (80 ha.), but the exact amount can only be
estimated, since there has been erosion on the western or
river side where the defences have totally disappeared. What

is of interest is the extension of the area enclosed by the earlier defences to include the land to the north of the Bell Brook. This could not have been merely to protect the water supply, which could equally well have been cut off to the east, but must have been for the protection of buildings. Although there are no signs of any stone foundations from air photographs, there appears to be evidence of timber structures. Thus *Viroconium* became one of the largest cities in the province, a testimony to its flourishing condition after such a hesitant start.

The reasons for its outstanding success are not obvious. Unlike Cirencester, there is no evidence of a wealthy countryside, nor, like the cities of the south, is there a sophisticated native culture. The answer may be found in its relationship to the military zone, for apart from Caerwent in south Wales, it is the only city offering any facilities to the troops on leave from the Welsh garrisons. The community came into being to provide legionaries with goods and services, and could well have continued in that tradition. *Viroconium* may even have competed with the *canabae* of Chester, where there is strangely little evidence of a large and flourishing civil settlement.

Nothing is known of the third century which in other parts of the province is thought in its second half to have been one of financial chaos, ruin and decay. Usually when the evidence is carefully examined it is found to have been stretched to fit the historical theory. Towards the end of the century there was certainly a currency crisis, which may have been responsible for the burying of so many hoards of coins,[52] and there was a movement of the western provinces to break away from the central authority. It is doubtful if this affected everyday life very much, but the ruling families may have suffered in loss of wealth or in political rivalry. The rich no longer felt obligations towards the maintenance of public buildings and monuments in the cities, and in consequence city centres probably began to take on a somewhat run-down appearance, although this was only a temporary lapse. Better times were ahead with the stabilisation of the Empire under Diocletian and the House of Constantine.

The fourth century

Before this could happen, however, there was a British
breakaway from the Empire under Carausius, a commander
of the British Fleet. His strong-arm rule in Britain from A.D.
283 to 294 appears to have been successful but that of his
murderer and successor, his finance officer, Allectus, was a
disaster. While Carausius remained in power, Diocletian and
his colleagues were content to leave matters, but they soon
saw that Britain could be regained by the ineptitude of
Allectus. So Constantius Chlorus crossed to Britain with a
large army in A.D. 296 and found the province in a state of
total civil disorder, swarming with brigands and rebels taking
what they could. After he had relieved London, Constantius
took steps to bring Britain under firm control. Archaeological
evidence for this phase of the recovery can be seen in a chain
of strong points (*burgi*) along Watling Street from London to
Wroxeter.[53] Control of this important route would effectively have divided the province into two parts, enabling his
forces to seal off the raiding parties to the south-west of the
line and prevent them from moving back to the north. As yet
only five of these strong points are known but they all have
similar features and defensive ditches and walls. Four are
dated to the early fourth century, but only by the absence of
later pottery.[54] Where they have been carefully studied it is
clear that the ditches of these defences were not left open for
very long and were filled in, presumably because they could
have been a danger to traffic. The trouble may have been
resolved quickly but the work was not carried out as a short
term expediency since there is evidence that the stone walls
were contemporary.[55] The walls may have been later
reduced in height, but were not entirely removed.[56] The
strategic importance of the site of *Viroconium* was once
more recognised by the army after a peaceful interval of two
hundred years, but by this time military occupation could
hardly have been even a faint memory. After all how many of
us have family recollections of the French Revolution or the
American War of Independence?

It is only in recent years that any useful evidence has
emerged of the city in the fourth century. There was a time

when the Roman towns were thought to have been in a state of decay and ironically enough *Viroconium* has produced indications of this in the forum excavations. The final destruction was dated by the excavator to the late third century.[57] This date was based on the finds of coins in the destruction deposits, although it was recognised that life continued since there were several periods of building over the levelled-off remains and a column drum which had fallen into the street had a deep rut worn in it. We now know that the bath-house also was out of commission by the early fourth century, but perhaps for a different reason. The building had been settling gradually into the sandy subsoil and had developed cracks, a serious matter in a structure dependent for its proper function on an efficient circulation of heat and an avoidance of the seepage of noxious fumes. The defects could have become so serious as to be beyond repair and a total rebuild was unthinkable. The *praefurnium* had also been relined so many times and its floor pro-gressively raised so much that it became difficult to operate; it might have been possible to construct a new furnace elsewhere, but the presence of the thick encasement wall would have made it virtually impossible. There is evidence of a flue with a boiler stand leading into the *tepidarium* on the east side and this could be explained as an attempt to keep the baths in commission by cutting off the south end which included the *caldarium* and main *praefurnium*. It may have been possible to continue for another generation the daily ritual for the dwindling number of citizens who still felt it to be part of the proper way of life.

So the loss of the two main civic buildings could be interpreted as a serious decline in civilised standards, but at this time there were considerable changes in social conditions and attitudes throughout the Empire. The palmy days of civic pride and patronage belong to the first two centuries of Imperial Rome, and the glories of the old Mediterranean tradition were gradually fading with the introduction of barbarian elements, mainly through army recruitment which drew more and more men from the frontier areas and beyond. Some outlying provinces like Britain were never as completely civilised as Gaul and in any case the cities with their temples, *fora* and *thermae* represent only the tip of a vast iceberg. The bulk of the population remained in the countryside virtually untouched by the policy of Romanisation, still living in their traditional Celtic manner. Society, by the fourth century, had become more rigid and wealth concentrated in the hands of fewer families. It is the time of the vast estates with their large country mansions and town houses, and it is against this kind of background that one must evaluate the decline in standards. When the two great public buildings at *Viroconium* needed a programme of rebuilding, they were instead allowed to collapse into ruins or were robbed of their fittings and stone. At the same time the local magnates were building their large town houses with their own bath-suites and perhaps with their own markets.

The bath-house at *Viroconium* became inhabited, doors were blocked up and a layer of grain on the floor of the *frigidarium* is evidence of its use as a store.[58] In the basilica there is a sequence of rough floors as people partitioned off the vast hall into dwelling areas. One might use the term squalor, but it was probably no worse than the conditions in which most of the townspeople had been living over the previous centuries. Excavations in Roman towns have concentrated too much on the large important buildings and neglected the hovels of the lower social orders. Excavators have also tended to dig too rapidly through the upper layers of what they thought was building debris down to the solid floors, and so cleared away the evidence of the late conversion of many public buildings into tenements. This happened to the bath-house in the nineteenth century; fortunately, areas of the basilica and the southern and eastern edges of the site were left untouched. The south service corridor, for example, has now been investigated and one can see how the roof collapsed on to the floor and where lead flashings or gutters were removed and melted down. The coins from this layer are all late third-century issues, many of which were still circulating widely in the early fourth century. The *praefurnium* waste dump had produced a large quantity of pottery but not a single piece of the recognisable fourth-century wares which are prolific elsewhere, especially on the basilica.

After the shocks of the collapse of the rule of the British

usurper Allectus and the military occupation under Constantius, peaceful conditions returned, and it is doubtful if the inhabitants of *Viroconium* were much troubled by the thoughts of raiders from the north and west. The loss of the daily routine of the bath-house was probably considered a more serious matter, but we are not sure how suddenly, or just when this happened. With the reorganisation of the northern frontier and the operations of the British Fleet in the Irish Sea, there was little to fear until *c.* A.D. 340 when events caused a sudden visit of Constans, and then followed a strengthening of coastal defences. More serious for Britain was the brief reign of Magnentius, who appears to have had personal connections with the province. This is suggested by the results of his defeat by Constantius II in A.D. 351. That highly suspicious and mean-minded Emperor sent, as his agent to Britain, an unpleasant character named Paul who earned the name *Catena* (the fetters) and according to Ammianus 'exceeded his instructions and, like a flood, suddenly overwhelmed the fortunes of many, making the way amid manifold slaughter and destruction'.[59] The effect on Britain of widespread seizure of estates, and death or imprisonment of many men of the leading families, could have been very serious, and inevitably led to a weakening of local government. Any sufferings the Cornovii endured may have been intensified in A.D. 360 when the Scots broke the peace and 'laid waste the regions near the frontiers, so that fear seized the provincials, weakened as they were by a mass of past calamities'.[60] Since the Scots were at that time inhabiting Ireland, it is likely that North Wales may have been one of these frontiers. Julian, at that time in Gaul, despatched Lupicinus with a light-armed mobile corps to deal with the situation in mid-winter. This he appears to have done quickly, so the threat may not have been very serious. The defences of the province were in good order and the sea-borne raiders constantly frustrated in their attempts to reach the plunder they knew existed in the cities. The only solution for them was a well planned and co-ordinated attack at several points at once, which would split the Roman defences. This temporary alliance was achieved in A.D. 367 with devastating effect for Britain, as we shall see in the last chapter.

3.

Communications and Urban Settlement

The system of roads imposed on the territory of the Cornovii owes its pattern to two basic factors, the course of the River Severn and Roman military strategy. The effect of the river and its crossing points on communications has already been discussed above (p. 5) but one must also assume that the river itself formed an important transport link. A legionary fortress would not have been sited here unless there had been access to the Bristol Channel, and there is little doubt that the main bulk supplies came this way. The Forest of Dean with its rich iron ores must have supplied Wroxeter as well as Gloucester with the raw materials needed for armaments and defensive equipment. There was timber for construction in plenty from the extensive forests on both sides of the river. Oil and wine from other parts of the Empire could have been shipped direct to Gloucester and thence up-stream to Wroxeter, but corn collected from the Britons in the form of an annual levy (*annona*) was normally directed to receiving depots not always in places convenient for the provincials.[1] The implication of the statement by Tacitus is that delivery would have been direct to the forts and fortresses.

Control of the river and its crossing points was vital in the conquest period and this was achieved by means of a road along the east bank. This probably continued all the way, in the original scheme, to Wroxeter. North of Worcester, however, it ceased to have much commercial use later and the main road turned towards Droitwich and the important saltings, thence north to Greensforge (fig. 19), after which its course is not known, but it is clearly aimed at Wroxeter. The

Fig. 19. The Roman road south of Greensforge, near Stourbridge

most important route was undoubtedly the link with the
south-east, which was later to be called Watling Street and
eventually became the greater London-Holyhead road,
engineered by Telford, who deviated from the Roman course
only at a few points to ease the gradient. One of these places
was Overley Hill, where the Roman alignment goes straight
over the high point, doubtless following its original military
setting-out line from one elevation to the next. A section cut
in 1962[2] showed the considerable post-Roman usage which
unexpectedly accounted for the upstanding *agger*. The
excavators had some difficulty in locating the succession of
three Roman roads and eventually found them 1.5 m. from
present ground level at the south end of their trench. It was
suspected that the Roman roads represent a later northerly
extension from the original route, but the interesting fact
that they had been laid in a trench may indicate that they
were part of the original scheme, when the Roman engineers
were concerned primarily with minimising the gradients.

This road marks the early advance towards central Wales *c.*
A.D. 50 with its line of camps and forts at Wall (*Letocetum*),[3] *Pennocrucium*[4] and *Uxacona*,[5] and marching
camps at Burlington[6] (above, p. 28), and remained the main
link with London and the south-east;[7] but there is a
significant branch road from *Pennocrucium* aimed in the
north-easterly direction at Chester, dating surely from the
establishment of a legionary fortress there.

The route followed by this north-south road from
Wroxeter has long been known[8] and a remarkable aerial
photograph taken by the R.A.F. in 1929 after a light fall of
snow shows the course at the crossing of the Roden at
Harcourt Mill,[9] where the road station of *Rutunium* should
be, about twelve Roman miles from *Viroconium*, according
to Iter II.[10] The only evidence of this settlement to date is
the box of pottery in the Shrewsbury Museum, picked up in
the early fifties. About a mile to the north of this site, two
milestones were found in 1812 in draining Moston Pool,[11]
but these were afterwards lost before reliable illustrations
could be made.

A road aligned towards the south-west from Middlewich
has been traced as far as the River Weaver.[12] It could thence

have proceeded to Whitchurch or direct to Wroxeter, but of the latter there is only a faint hint in the parish boundaries and modern lanes at Ightfield.

The other important route from *Viroconium* has already been mentioned in connection with the conquest (p. 28). This is the road which links the Severn with the Wye and must have been a frontier road from which Ostorius Scapula tried so unsuccessfully to subjugate the Silures. Finally, there is the other military road plunging into the heart of central Wales up the Severn Valley to the forts at Forden Gaer and Caersws, which was a nodal point for the routes controlling this great central mountain massif.

This pattern gives us an extremely sketchy outline of the road system with only a few of the main routes being known. A glance at the Ordnance Survey map of Roman Britain gives some immediate indication of several other possibilities and some of these lines have been ably explored on the ground by Dr. A.W.J. Houghton. There are two roads in Herefordshire which could be continued northwards from Blackwardine and from Stretton Grandison. The first of these has been followed by Dr. Houghton to the point where it joins Watling Street West at Marshbrook.[13] The road which can be followed so firmly by modern roads up to Stretton Grandison can only be projected to Much Cowarne, but if the general alignment is continued it may join the other road somewhere near Woofferton, where some strange crop-marks recorded by Mr. Arnold Baker may indicate an unusual site, which is not yet dated.[14]

An important east-west route also studied by Dr. Houghton[15] is that known as the Hen Ffordd (the old road), which linked Greensforge with Forden Gaer, crossing the main north-south road at Craven Arms with a fort and marching camp[16] indicating a key site in the early campaigns. The alignment must also approximate to an earlier trackway, since it passes by Norton Camp, Wart Hill, Billings Ring, The Roveries and Castle Ring and the large number of mediaeval fortified sites is testimony of its continued usage. A farm at the eastern end of the road near Claverley has the interesting name of Winchester, which may have been derived from the Celtic *venta* (a market or place of assembly). If one considers a further possible route from Wall Town, it would make Craven Arms a nodal point where one might expect a small settlement, but the only hint of this at present is the discovery of a chatelaine at Stokesay. To the north-east is a main military route running parallel to Watling Street.[17] It appears to spring from the Fosse at *Vernemetum* and links Littlechester, Rocester, Chesterton, and Middlewich and thence continues to the north.

The network as at present so imperfectly known (fig. 20) leaves enormous gaps, like that in the rectangle Wroxeter, Caersws, Caer Gai and Chester. There must surely have been a route up to the Tanat Valley joining Wroxeter with Caer Gai, and parish boundaries give a hint of an alignment from the crossing of the Severn near Montford Bridge through Wilcott to Kinnerley. Such a road would have been necessary for the transport of copper from the Llanymynech mines, and may also have had another connection with Caersws along the north side of the valley of the Vyrnwy, as suggested by Nash-Williams,[18] possibly continuing towards Malpas. One might also speculate on the need for a road south from *Viroconium* to communicate with the fort at Wall Town, which at present stands in total isolation. Field work and aerial reconnaissance will bring rich rewards. There are also the hints to follow up in early documents, such as the Anglo-Saxon boundary charters. A high street is mentioned in Ape Dale running on a north-south alignment through Paish,[19] and the same charter includes the stone quarry on Hoar Edge which supplied *Viroconium* with some of its stone. A paved road known as the Devil's Causeway, a name often evidence of a pre-Saxon origin, could have joined Watling Street at Acton Burnell. A chance discovery here led to the investigation of an interesting Roman bridge with embankments over a small ravine, thought to have been necessary for avoiding steep gradients in a route used by carts heavily laden with stone.[20]

The communication network was clearly the work of the Roman Army and belongs to the conquest period of the first century. Its aim was to control large areas and enable the rapid movement and deployment of troops. The military needs remained paramount over much of the area through-

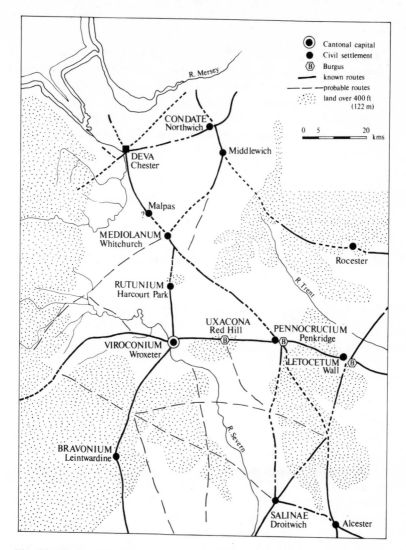

Fig. 20. Roman roads, urban sites and *burgi* in the canton of the Cornovii

out, but with pacification and the growth of urban settlement, the roads became used for civil transport and travel. Goods concentrated in the principal markets and all but *Viroconium* would have been minor centres. Heavy loads of pottery were moved along Watling Street from the large factory at *Manduessedum* and luxury goods came from the

London warehouses. The development of the mineral resources of lead, silver and copper necessitated additional
roads and, as seen above, the vast quantity of building
materials needed in the capital city must have required well
engineered routes for the transport of heavy loads. The
countryside too must have had its minor tracks linking the
villas and farmsteads with the main routes, all of which
indicates how much still needs to be done not only in finding
the roads themselves, but establishing a chronology for their
origin and development.

The tribal capital

The splendid new city of *Viroconium* was laid out on the
area of the demolished fortress. The alignment of the new
street plan in the typical Roman grid pattern is the same as
that of the military buildings, so it is possible that one of the
main streets of the fortress (*via principalis*) became the main
north-south street of the city, and excavations will one day
demonstrate if this is a mere speculation. In the centre of the
city large and imposing public buildings were planned. On the
west side of the street were to be public baths and opposite
them the forum. As discussed above (p. 41), there is evidence
of the construction of public buildings *c.* A.D. 90, but after
an auspicious beginning, things went wrong. The total area
occupied by the baths was 81 m. by 124 m. At the front was
a large open *palaestra* or exercise area 76 m. by 56 m. with a
colonnade on all four sides. The baths themselves were
elaborately equipped with the usual heated rooms including
two *laconica* (dry heat) and a large central *frigidarium* (cold
room) with cold plunges at each end. It would have been one
of the finest bath-houses in Roman Britain, but it was never
completed.[21]

It is reasonable to assume that the great public buildings
on the other side of the road would have been planned as the
forum. Excavations have revealed early walls which do not
belong to the later bath-house and some of these were
incorporated into the later structure. It was suggested by Miss
Kenyon that the basilica of the later baths was originally
planned as that of the forum,[22] but there are two difficulties

here. Firstly this would leave insufficient space on the north side, between the hall and the street, for a suite of offices, and secondly this arrangement would place the main entrance on the south side, whereas it ought to be on the west side of the site on the main street. Too little is at present known to permit further discussion, but it is possible that further evidence of the plan of pre-bath structures may yet emerge from the present series of excavations.

The city centre however remained almost unoccupied, looking like a derelict building site, and so the bright hopes for the new city faded. It may be, as with some of the new towns of today, that the inhabitants were reluctant to move from their existing homes near the river. Things did not begin to move again until *c.* 125, when new decisions were taken, architects became busy with their plans, and for some reason, possibly a change from military to civilian ideas, the sites were switched round. The new forum was to be built on the abandoned baths and *vice versa*. Not only were many old foundations re-used, but some of the stones intended for the bath-house were incorporated in the new structure. Cornice mouldings and other architectural features can be seen forming the stylobate of the forum colonnade along the street, which is now exposed to view.

By good fortune fragments of most of a fine inscription at the entrance to the forum were found where it had collapsed into the street when the building fell into ruin. This is one of the most beautifully cut inscriptions ever to have been found in Britain and enough has survived to complete it with certainty. It records the dedication of the forum, in the reign of Hadrian, by the tribe of the Cornovii. The slab, of a local fine grained sandstone, is 3.59 m. by 1.14 m. and has been set up in the Rowley House Museum, with a cast in the museum on the site (fig. 18). The lettering must have been cut by a skilled craftsman brought from Gaul or possibly practising in London, where unfortunately no similar inscriptions have survived for comparison.[23] It can be dated precisely to A.D. 130 by reference to the emperor's fourteenth year of tribunician power, and mounted on the pediment over the entrance, it presumably dates the completion of the work. So at last *Viroconium* was provided with the basic essentials of any city, a market place and 'town-hall' where the tribal council (*ordo*) met, where justice was done according to the Roman law and where the permanent officials had their offices. The building occupied precisely the same site as the unfinished baths, and its plan was that normally found in Roman Britain, bearing a striking resemblance to that of the military head-quarters (*principia*).

The forum (fig. 21) is a large building occupying almost 2.5 acres (1 ha.) divided into two distinct parts. The market-place was an open area 74 m. by 70 m. with colonnades on three sides and the great hall or basilica on the west side. This had a nave 12 m. wide and two aisles of 4.7 m., and attached to it on the west was a range of five main rooms, which would have served as offices for the tribal authority. The northernmost of these rooms produced some interesting evidence of use as an office or an archive. To quote Atkinson, there were 'many pieces of iron including four rectangular lock-plates with L-shaped keyholes, two padlocks, two large lock-bolts with springs, three keys, three handles with split staples, four pairs of split staples joined by oval links, four similar but with round links, three pairs of hinges and two odd ones and a collection of nails'. His conclusion was that it had all belonged to lockable chests or cupboards. The most important object from this room was part of a bronze military diploma, or discharge certificate, issued in A.D. 135 to a man whose name may have been Mansuetus, of the second cohort of Dalmatians, and whose father was a citizen of Trier. Where this unit was stationed in Britain in the second century is not known, but later it was at Carvoran on the Wall according to the *Notitia* (xl, 43). Atkinson, in a rare moment of speculation, suggested that this man was actually the clerk employed here after his discharge from the army. All one can assume is that this important document, proving citizenship, must have been deposited by the man or his family in this office or archive. The most puzzling evidence from the forum is the central cross-colonnade which divides the market place into two parts. As this is based on the earlier bath-house walls, it requires further examination and consideration, as also does the curved foundation which does not relate satisfactorily to

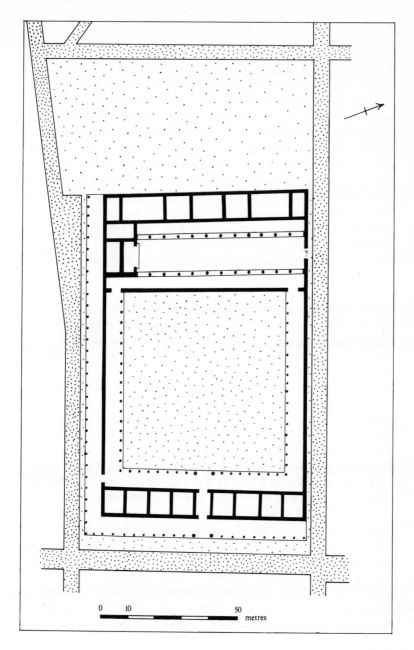

Fig. 21. Plan of the Wroxeter Forum

the plans of either the forum or the baths. For this reason these features are omitted from the plan (fig. 21).

It would be logical to assume that development under Hadrian also proceeded on the other derelict site on the opposite side of the road and this may be true of the building fronting the street and the colonnade. This was planned as a whole for the full width of the *insula* and as the ground slopes away to the south, that end had to be built up. This was done with domestic rubbish. When this was excavated from below the *macellum* floor in 1974 it was found to contain pieces of decorated samian of *c.* A.D. 100-125. The bath-house, however, was completed later since the dating evidence indicates that it was not in use until *c.* 160. A community consisting of retired legionaries and Gallic traders would hardly have liked to be without a public bath-house all these years, and there may have been one in the civil settlement, or inside the legionary fortress, which had been left standing for the use of the citizens. The evidence from Exeter seems to indicate that by the mid first century a large stone and tile bath-house was part of the legionary fortress, and if it had become military practice in Britain by *c.* A.D. 50, *Viroconium* would also have been provided with one.

The date of the first civil occupation along the main street is difficult to assess. Bushe-Fox, excavating along the west side, south of the forum, found a series of rectangular buildings with timber and daub walls and concrete floors. They were open-fronted to the street and were probably shops, with dwelling space at the rear or above. The pottery associated with this development was given the wide bracket of A.D. 80-120 and this led the excavator to the general opinion that these buildings belong to the early second century. It is probable that the date of the very first occupation given in his report as A.D. 80-90, is in fact that of the demolition of the fortress,[24] although the evidence of metallurgy may belong to the construction of the early baths.

The great fire of *c.* A.D. 160 destroyed the timber part of the forum and swept down the west side of the main street to the south. In the rebuilding a change of function and ownership took place in the properties, and in place of a row of shops a small temple was built,[25] dated by the layer of

Fig. 22. Wroxeter. Walls of a pre-baths building below the eastern
laconicum

burning below it and a foundation deposit in a black
burnished cooking pot.[26] Other buildings may have been
associated with this temple, forming a *tempelbezirk* like
those on the Rhine,[27] and included a priest's house, with a
shop on the street for selling votive objects and a workshop
behind it to produce them. A small bath-house was attached
at the rear of the temple, possibly related to ritual cleansing,
and there was also a large hall where the officers and devotees
of the cult could assemble and don their robes and regalia.
The most enigmatic structure found by Bushe-Fox was the
rectangular enclosure in the area to the west of the temple.[28]
The only reasonable explanation of it is that it was an arena,
surrounded by a wall to support timber seating, and its
proximity to the temple permits a further suggestion that it
was for religious purposes. A similar relationship exists at
Caerwent with the siting of the so-called amphitheatre[29] and
the temple-complex fronting the main street.

About this time, and perhaps prompted by this wholesale
rebuilding, work was started once more on the other large
insula opposite the forum which up to now had remained
derelict. The planning of this *insula* is unusual for Britain and
may have been influenced by the presence of earlier walls,
some of the foundations of which were re-used (fig. 22). The
greater part of it was taken up by the bath-house (figs. 23,
24) which appears on the plan in the form of an inverted L.
The main entrance from the street gives access to the great
covered *palaestra* or basilica, about 73 m. long and 21 m.
wide (somewhat larger than the Hall of Westminster Palace),
with service rooms at the east end and external colonnades
along the street flanking the west and north sides. Massive
columns estimated to have been 8.5 m. high supported the
nave, which had a span of 9.14 m. The upstanding masonry, a
miraculous survival known as the 'Old Work', was part of the
south wall and it still stands today to its full original height
of almost 8 m. One can calculate from this that the apex of
the nave roof may have been as much as 15 m. above ground
level. Tessellated pavements were found in the nineteenth-
century excavations along the north aisle and parts of them
removed.[30] The nave and south aisle were covered with small
tiles set on edge in a herring-bone pattern. The apparent lack

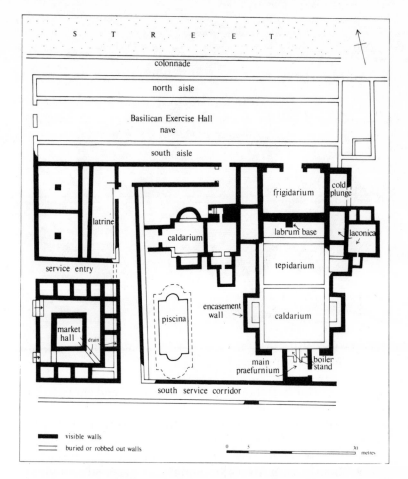

Fig. 23 Wroxeter. The public baths

of consistency may have been the result of reflooring, or there may have been lengths of the north aisle which were partitioned for offices.

This great structure was the exercise hall of the bath-house, where the citizens played their games, did their physical jerks or watched others, and judging from the quantity of animal bones dumped outside the building also indulged in eating. The remains were mixed with floor sweepings from which were recovered many pieces of broken jewellery, including pins, rings and beads and spacers from jet

Fig. 24. A reconstruction, by Alan Sorrell, of the baths in their first period, from the south

necklaces. The bath-house was at the east end and at right angles to the hall, and entered through double doors in the 'Old Work'. A close study of this stonework shows the emplacements of the monolithic stone jambs and lintels which have been removed.[31] The first room was the *frigidarium* (cold room), with its cold plunges at each side, and the bather could have proceeded thence either into the humid, warm room (*tepidarium*) and then into the hot wet room (*caldarium*) or into the pair of hot dry rooms (*laconica*) of which there was one on each side of the cold room. The hot-wet block was a massive structure 35 m. by 17.9 m., roofed with a great barrel vault of mass concrete lightened with tufa lumps. Its internal width of 14.5 m. was probably the height of the inside of the roof from the springing of the arch, giving a total height of about 18.3 m. This enormous group of rooms would have held several hundred bathers at any one time. The building had been so badly wrecked in antiquity that it is difficult to reconstruct its internal appearance, but fragments found in the excavation indicate

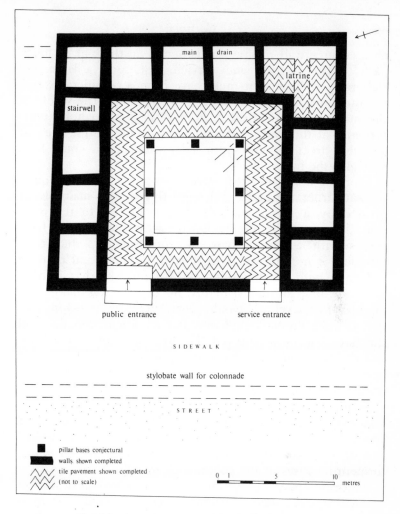

Fig. 25. Wroxeter. The market hall (*macellum*)

that the floors were covered with tessellated pavements and walls with plaster painted in bold geometric designs, probably to give the impression of coffering in the distant ceiling. The subsoil of the site is soft sand and the erection of such a heavy structure must have given much concern to the builders, although the main walls were five feet thick at base and the foundations ten feet below ground level. Before it was even completed, settlement took place and cracks began to appear, and the whole of the block was immediately encased in a wall of grey sandstone, 3 m. thick at its lower part.[32] The heating and servicing of such a large and elaborate establishment must have been a considerable task for the baths manager and his corps of slaves. The whole of the main block was heated from a single stoke-hole (*prae-furnium*) at the south end with access to the yard to the east and the street on the south side, where carts could have unloaded the fuel.

Fronting the main street were other public buildings, quite separate from the baths and consisting of two main blocks divided by a passageway which gave access to the open central area and the *piscina.* On the west side were two large rooms with a central base for roof supports, but their function is not known. Wright records some kind of oven associated with metal working, but from his sketch[33] it looks as if the base of the structure he depicts was below the original floor level and would seem, therefore, to belong to a period when the building had ceased its original function and the floor had been removed. To the rear of the two rooms, and divided from them by a passageway or eavesdrip, was a large latrine entered on the east side by a door from the north-south colonnade.

South of the central passage is a complete market-hall (*macellum*), a massive structure with a central gravelled court, flanked on three sides by colonnades which had herring-bone tile floors (fig. 25). The large stones which formed the bases of the columns clearly show that there was at least one upper storey. The colonnade surrounded a series of small square rooms which must have had wooden floors at the level of, or slightly higher than, the tile pavement; these were presumably shops and offices. In the south-east corner of the court was a drain to take the rainwater from the roofs, and this led into a latrine with a herring-bone floor two feet lower than the court. The drain led into another which appears to have flowed north to the other latrine and into a main drain under the south aisle of the basilica, where a sewer is noted 'so large that one might creep up it from some distance each way'.[34] One of the strange features of these drains, which will receive comment below, is how thoroughly they have all been robbed of their tiles. The market-hall was entered direct from the main street through a colonnade which ran along its west-side. The floor of the court and colonnades is three feet above the paving outside, and this necessitated a flight of steps, only the lowest course of which survives, leading into the north side of the market. At the south end there is another but narrower entrance. This building at floor level and below survives to a remarkable extent and had not received serious damage in the nineteenth-century excavations or subsequently. At the time of writing it is being excavated and the substantial remains, when fully excavated, will help to give a better understanding of the history of the *insula*. Walls of an earlier building, but of a different plan, are already evident.

The uncertainty which surrounds the history of this *insula* is due to the thorough excavations of the last century. The site was also left open to the vagaries of the weather and over-curious visitors of earlier generations, who have removed almost all the traces of hypocaust pillars in many of the rooms. On the east side of the site is a large open area doubtless used as a storage space for fuel and for dumping furnace waste. This contains not only ash but also building materials from the periodic relining of the main furnace and repairs to the structure. The deposit is 1.5 m. thick in places, and excavations have produced a large quantity of pottery, not one single piece of which can be dated later than the third century.

A major reorganisation of the baths was undertaken in the early third century, with the addition of a new and self-contained bath-block on the west side of the main block. The reason for this extension of the bath facilities is not obvious and there are several possibilities. It may have been done to cope with an increase in population, or to provide a private suite for a privileged group such as a merchants' guild. Alternatively it may have been intended for women, who normally had to bathe in the late morning before the baths were generally open. Finally, the extension may have been necessary when the main block had to undergo extensive repairs which might have put it out of action for a long time. This reorganisation of the baths was partly achieved by a conversion of the west *laconicum* suite into a *tepidarium*, and

Fig. 26. The *piscina* with its few surviving floor slabs, and fragments of the concrete surround seen as standing blocks

by adding a *caldarium* with a semi-circular apse on its north side, and a rectangular one on the south. The *praefurnium* to the west backed onto the north-south colonnade. All this necessitated the replanning of the open area round the *piscina*, to which access was now cut from the basilica. The pool was dismantled, the fine floor and side slabs were prised out (fig. 26) and all the architectural features demolished, leaving an untidy sunken area which was promptly filled in with city rubbish. This deposit has some interesting features; the layers of rubbish alternate with clean sand, showing that some attempt was made to prevent an unpleasant stench. These layers produced a remarkable collection of domestic pottery and animal bones, but not a single coin or metal object. The pottery forms a useful late second-century group and includes a quantity of plain samian, suggesting a date for the deposit of *c.* A.D. 210.[35] This radical change of plan also affected the colonnades round the *piscina*, and although there are still problems to be resolved, it looks as if they were converted into service corridors, but preserving public access to the main latrine. Since the robber trenches of the walls of the *piscina* cut through the rubbish deposit, this probably took place after the building went out of use as a bath-house,

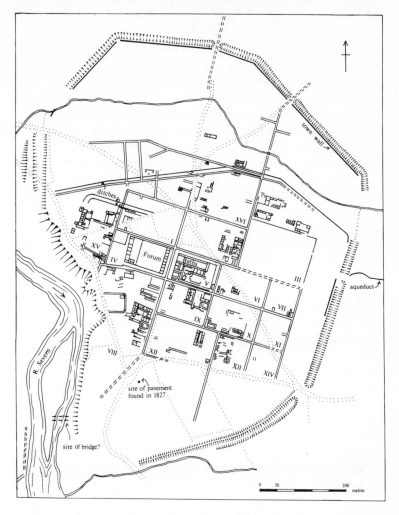

Fig. 27. Plan of *Viroconium* (Wroxeter)

possibly when all the tile linings of the drains were also robbed.

There is, however, one important public building still missing from the plan of the city and its environs — the amphitheatre, which was a prime source of entertainment. If it exists outside the city it has not so far been recognised on the ground or from the air. Even had it been thoroughly robbed, and levelled for agriculture, there should be distinctive traces to be found of such a large and massive structure, but it may have been a much slighter affair, like the one already noted at Caerwent, or that at Chichester.[36]

The sand and gravel subsoil over the whole of the area of the city, except in the southern sector, make it very suitable for differentials in crop growth. Foundations and ditches below ground are reflected in the growth of crops on the surface in a dry season by differing rates of growth and ripening. *Viroconium* has produced over the years some of the most remarkable photographs of a buried city, making it possible to plot many streets and buildings and to draw a plan without carrying out any excavations (fig. 27). It must, however, be realised that at most only about twenty per cent of the structures can ever be recorded in this way, and that one sees only those features nearest the surface. What lies deeper and constitutes the early history of the site can be revealed only by large scale excavation.

A glance at the plan immediately raises the basic questions about the origins and growth of the city.[37] The central area has a regular grid of streets, but to the north and west anomalies are present which can only be accounted for by an extension of the original plan in developments of a later date. Little shows from the air in the southern part of the city, due to the change in the subsoil from sand to clay, but one has only to walk over the ground after ploughing to see the wide scatter of building and occupation material. The south-western part of this area may eventually produce the answers to the early civil history, since there it may include part of the *canabae* on the road south of the fortress. Most of the buildings recorded from crop-marks are houses, some of them quite substantial. The largest is beyond the north-west corner of the forum and covers an area about 61 m. by 107 m. A small temple lies north of the central grid and fragments of a domestic shrine have also been found in the city (fig. 28). Perhaps the most interesting and puzzling area is to the east of this, where the highest part of the site includes a very large enclosure. Larger than any *insula* (200 m. by 150 m.) it appears to be devoid of any building, although there are good crop-marks on the west and north sides.

An essential service to a civilised community in Roman

Fig. 28. Reconstruction of a domestic shrine from Wroxeter

Fig. 29. The Wroxeter aqueduct, under snow, before it was filled in

times was a good and constant water supply, and all the cities and main towns must have had aqueducts. They were normally modest embanked channels built on the ground, carefully laid out to a suitable gradient to enable the water to flow by gravity. The great arched stone structures of other provinces occur where either a deep valley had to be crossed or, as at Rome, the flat plain made height necessary to give the required gradient. This was never necessary in Britain, so there were only the small leats or channels, most of which have disappeared with levelling and ploughing long since. A length of the aqueduct at *Viroconium* was still visible only a few years ago (fig. 29), but this was, alas, bulldozed away to make for more efficient farming.

The source of the water supply was the Bell Brook, and at a point three-quarters of a mile to the west of the city there is a small valley which could have been made for a reservoir. A succession of crop-marks shows the line of the channel winding its way along the contours at a gradient of 0.68 m. per mile. A section cut in 1958 showed that the channel was

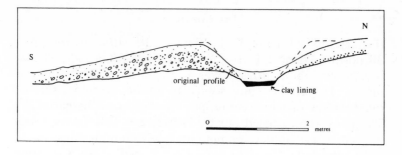

Fig. 30. Section through the aqueduct at Wroxeter

about 2.4 m. wide at the top and 0.9 m. deep (fig. 30). With
some reasonable assumptions made from the original cross-
section, a foot of water would have given a discharge of
almost two million gallons a day.[38] The channel would have
had special arrangements to carry it across the defences and
the best solution would have been to provide an entrance
with a causeway across the ditch system. Once inside the
city, it would have followed the street system, probably with
cover slabs to prevent pollution. Fountains would have been
constructed at selected points and the system soon began to
branch out to cover different sections of the city. One of
these branches would have led direct to the baths where a
great quantity of water would have been used daily. The
water would also be used to flush drains and latrines and at
these points the supply would turn into sewers. Evidence of
supplies to private properties was found by Bushe-Fox along
the main street. The water channel ran along the edge of the
street and there were leads into the houses with vertical slots
near the junctions, where boards could be raised and lowered
when the supply was needed. A complex system of drainage
must have existed under the city, taking all the waste to the
river and discharging it at some convenient point, but as yet
very little is known about it.

Minor urban settlements

After Wroxeter the most important settlement was at
Whitchurch (*Mediolanum*) half way to Chester. The name
Mediolanum is a fairly common one for towns in the Roman
world, the most famous example being Milan. It is very apt in

the case of Whitchurch, in view of its siting in the great
Shropshire Plain.[39] Until the excavations of 1965-6, all that
was known about the site was a few scattered finds summed
up by Haverfield; 'this seems to point to some sort of
inhabitation of which more may be discovered hereafter'.[40]
The excavation carried out by Professor G.D.B. Jones[41] was
limited to a small development area, with serious problems of
spoil disposal. Nevertheless, it produced some surprising
results which make it all the more necessary to ensure that
no further development takes place without time for full
scale excavations. There were very clear indications of
military activity before A.D. 75, probably in conjunction
with the establishment of the legionary fortress at Wroxeter.
This was succeeded by a definite fort *c.* A.D. 75 connected,
no doubt, with the consolidation following the conquest of
Brigantia. Part of the western defences of this fort was found,
and traces of internal buildings. The army remained here
until *c.* A.D. 90 and the site was handed over to the civil
authorities at the time *Legio XX* moved to Chester.

The remains of civil occupation were more difficult to
interpret. The High Street is clearly on the Roman road
through the town, but the nearest part of the excavated area
to this was 30 m. away. One might have expected little but
outbuildings and gardens here, and this seems to have been
true of the early period, which is represented by timber
buildings with small scale industrial activity. But the situation
was totally changed at some time not earlier than *c.* A.D.
170,[42] when the town was expanding to such an extent that
substantial stone buildings appear. The plan of only one of
these, Building I, was recovered sufficiently to allow any
opinion of its general appearance to be formed. There were
three ranges of small rooms arranged round a central court
with an ambulatory, the overall width of the building being
estimated at about 83 m. It could have been part of a
court-yard house, but the regular planning may reflect a
public function such as small market-hall.[43] The adjacent
building (No. III) is on the same alignment but too little of it
was recovered to establish any firm relationship between the
buildings, either in function or date; nor could much be said
of the later history since subsequent interference had

removed almost all the floor levels.[44] A fragment of wall with a corner, designated as Building II, was thought to have superseded Building I, but the evidence is not wholly convincing, and it could have been an addition forming an external corridor. Unfortunately, a baulk obscures the relationship between these buildings and a yard, the surface of which produced some fourth-century pottery. Difficulties arose in interpreting the industrial processes, including a brine kiln, which followed these buildings. These structures, cut into the robbed-out Roman walls, indicated a clear break with this earlier period. There was, however, no dating evidence, the only pottery found was Roman and probably all residual. A very odd discovery below the presumed floor of Building II was that of an inhumation of a young man whose skull had been expertly trephined, an operation practiced in classical times to relieve head pains. Pottery found with the skeleton was dated to the early fourth century,[45] but it is very unusual to find burials in Roman settlements, even in the fourth century. The skilled trepanation does, however, make it difficult to place it in a post-Roman context.

The small town of *Letocetum* (Wall, near Lichfield), on Watling Street, owed its origins to the military presence on the ridge of sandstone which rises sharply above the plateau and offers extensive views to the west. A succession of sites, beginning with marching camps[46] followed by the fortress of *Legio XIV*, mark this place as one of considerable importance to the army in the first century.[47] They were evidently reluctant to leave, since the last fort of the series is one of only half an acre, held into the early second century as a signal station or guard post along this vital route. The name appears in both the Antonine Itinerary[48] (470,2) and the Ravenna Cosmography[49] (No. 94) and means 'grey wood', and in the Welsh form, Caer Lwytgoed, has been transferred to Lichfield. The modern name 'Wall' appears to have been derived from a long stretch of masonry visible at least up to 1817 in the field known as Castle Croft, and which was presumably part of the late defence system discussed below.

Although a good deal of investigation has been carried out on the site, very little is as yet known about the civil

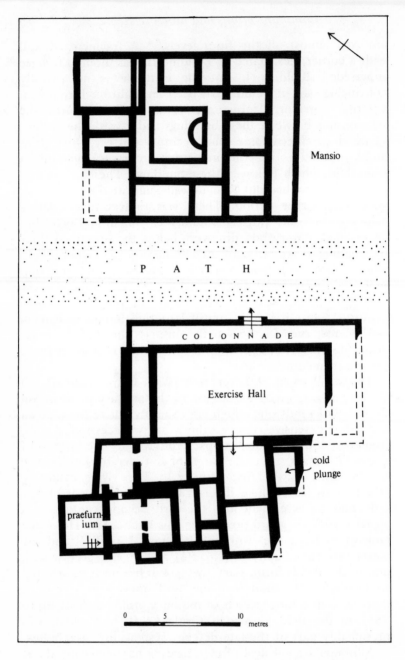

Mansio

P A T H

C O L O N N A D E

Exercise Hall

cold plunge

praefurnium

0   5   10
metres

Fig. 31. Wall (*Letocetum*). The *mansio* and baths

settlement. It was a two-mile ribbon strip of development along the main road and occupation has been noted at points along this length.[50] A mile to the east, the road crossed a peat bog and a building was even found on this unsuitable subsoil.[51] Where the modern village stands there are more substantial buildings between the ridge and the little stream to the west, and beyond this is the cemetery. Two buildings are known in some detail (fig. 31), the bath-house and a courtyard house, and since they clearly form a planned unit, as at Godmanchester,[52] it has been assumed that the latter was the *mansio*. The buildings are on different levels and their relationship is based on terraces in the hill slope with a metalled road or yard between them held by a retaining wall in which there was an ornamental gateway.

At present only something of the history of the bath-house is known; although this was excavated in 1912-14[53] and left exposed, enough remained to offer a chronology in a more recent investigation.[54] A small part of the foundations of an early bath-house was found on the same alignment but of quite a different plan; this had the appearance of an unfinished building. The dating evidence was slight but placed it not before the late first century, but whether this was an early civil bath-house or a late military one, it is not possible to judge on present evidence. The bath-house which later came into being was a modest one but its construction remains undated. Considerable alterations and additions were made in the early third century or maybe later. There were a number of further alterations and eventually the main flue had to be replaced with a new one which involved some internal reorganisation of the rooms. The visible remains, on what is now a guardianship site of the Department of the Environment, form a very complicated sequence of walls and floors which cannot be fully understood. On the east side is the exercise area, at first an open space but later roofed over. In its final form some of the doors were blocked, suggesting that when the building ceased to function as a bath-house, it was divided into small tenements. The other building on the east side and at a higher level has been known as the 'Villa'. It is a small courtyard house with colonnades on its south and western sides. A large-scale excavation, being planned in

1974, may reveal its history. Work on the bath-house has already postulated the presence of an early timber building which was destroyed by fire.

Letocetum was one of the sites along Watling Street selected as a strong-point when the army regained control of Britain under Constantius Chlorus (above p. 46). The defences consisted of three ditches separated by a 2 m. berm from a stone wall 3 m. thick with rounded corners. The enclosure of six acres (2.4 ha.) makes it one of the largest of the series.[55] Like the others it appears to contain no substantial buildings. The amount of dating evidence is slight,[56] but it seems to indicate the early fourth century. An unfinished well was found below the wall on the west side and in this was found fragments of a white jar with painted lettering and although there are fourteen letters which should refer to the contents, the meaning remains enigmatic.[57]

Very little is known about the other two small road side settlements between Wall and Wroxeter. Their Roman names, *Pennocrucium* and *Uxacona*, are given in the Antonine Itinerary. The former means 'place by the chief mound or hill'[58] which could signify a special assembly point for the tribe, or a place of some local importance, and the latter means 'high place'[59] which suits it very well. Some work has been done at *Pennocrucium*, but the results have not produced anything very definite in the form of buildings or stratification,[60] apart from the late defences.[61]

4.

Rural Settlement

The main wealth of the Cornovian territory was, as it is now, in the rich and varied agriculture which it supported. The extent to which the land was used in the Roman period is still subject to discovery and investigation. Because Shropshire has not produced examples of the large and well-appointed villa it has been too readily assumed that the countryside as a whole was poorly developed. There is undoubtedly a scatter of farms to be recorded in the Shropshire Plain when it can be closely studied from the air and on the ground, but by now the massive stone foundations of villas would have been encountered by the plough in a county where farming has been energetically pursued for centuries. One must be resigned to the fact that few establishments of this type await discovery.

This brings us to the suggestion of Sir Ian Richmond[1] that, due to the proximity of lawless terrain, the great tribal landowners lived in *Viroconium* and left their estates to the peasantry and their bailiffs. This is an interesting idea, but there is no evidence of any unrest in the area until the middle of the fourth century. A case for a British uprising in Wales at the end of the second century has been made by Dr. Grace Simpson[2] and developed later, with a statement that 'Forden Gaer was destroyed several times by enemy hands and the forum at Wroxeter was twice destroyed'.[3] The evidence from Forden Gaer is derived from a few trenches cut in 1927-9,[4] and with the experience we now have of area excavations, one is reluctant to draw any conclusion from evidence of such poor quality. A 'thin burnt layer' seen in a narrow trench can hardly be seriously considered as evidence of a catastrophe, since burning can have been caused by several means, including ovens, cooking hearths and peaceful demolition. As noted above there is no basis for the assumption that part of *Viroconium* was destroyed by external agencies in the second or the fourth centuries. The other evidence which Dr. Simpson has used to support her theory is epigraphic. An inscription from Caernarvon refers to the restoration of the channels of an aqueduct which 'collapsed through age',[5] and it is Dr. Simpson's contention that this is a deliberate official effort to disguise destruction by enemy action. There are certainly cases where this could have happened but it seems unlikely that the Britons would have wrecked a water channel which was no more than a small leat leading water into the fort from a distant spring. A period of military abandonment would, however, have necessitated such a restoration and there is considerable evidence, from a study of the pottery, of the deliberate evacuation of some of the Welsh forts,[6] and this could be equally well seen as a period of peace during which the troops could more effectively have been used elsewhere.

If one studies the Ordnance Survey Map of Roman Britain, the density of sites and finds in Cornovian territory appears no less than in most of the other similar areas; less than some parts of Brigantia perhaps but considerably more than Dumnonia (fig. 32). The distribution of villas so dramatically demonstrated by Mr. Rivet in 1955[7] shows how few there are north and west of the Trent and lower Severn, and those of the Cornovii compare favourably in density with those to the south. The lands of the Cornovii, like those of the other peoples beyond the limits of the original province, were cultivated by peasant communities little affected by Romanisation. It may be worthy of note that in the whole of the silt Fens, a vast area intensively cultivated at this period, there is hardly a single villa.[8] The situation, therefore, has nothing to do with security or unrest, but represents a way of life with crops and stock, and some hunting and fishing, typical of most Celtic peoples, but as yet little studied or understood in detail. It is not surprising, therefore, that it is so difficult to decide whether their occupation sites belong to the late Iron

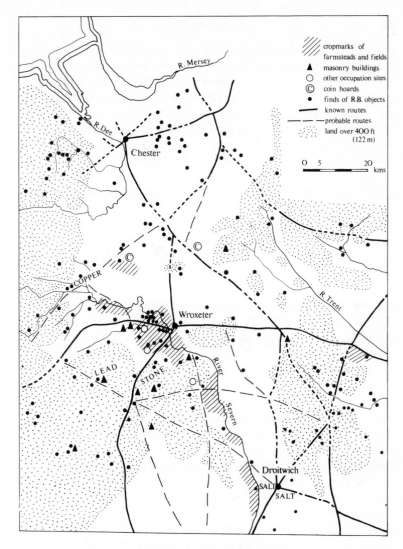

Fig. 32. Rural and industrial sites in the canton

Age or the Roman period. But there is no longer a problem if one admits the probability of a continuity of this way of life with changes only in land ownership and taxation.

There is, however, another aspect which may be important. While *Viroconium* did not become a *colonia* for retired veterans like Lincoln and Gloucester, her links with the army persisted. The retired legionaries who settled down with their fellow-soldiers still in service may have invested their savings and bounties in the land and established a tradition of a military land-owning class. An indication of this possibility can be seen in the discovery of three military *diplomatae* in the territory. These discharge certificates in the form of inscribed bronze plates were important documents, giving proof of the owners' citizenship and honourable discharge. That of Mansuetus (?) of *Coh. II Dalmatiorum*, dated to A.D. 135 and found in the Wroxeter Forum, has already been considered (p. 58). That of Reburrus, a Spaniard, *decurio* of *Ala Pannoniorum Tampiana*, dated to A.D. 103, was found near Malpas in 1812 and is now in the British Museum.[9] The third, of an unknown trooper of *Ala Classiana civium Romanorum* and dated to A.D. 105, was found at Middlewich in 1939.[10] The Wroxeter find may have been in the city's archive and that from Middlewich from a house in *Salinae*, but the example from Malpas is not near any known settlement, and may have been found on the site of this man's farm. There is here a case for the supposition that auxiliaries discharged in the early second century were settling down with their families in Cornovian territory and becoming farmers or going into business. The deliberate settlement of veterans in frontier areas was a policy developed by Hadrian; no longer were old soldiers grouped together in *coloniae* but they were now encouraged to own lands behind the frontiers. This policy compliments that which the Emperor introduced for recruitment, which was made entirely provincial with better promotion prospects.[11] Hadrian's concept was that of a citizen militia, ready to protect the lands its members owned. What may have survived of the Celtic aristocracy among the Cornovii may have been superseded by the newcomers, all military men but all provincials themselves, and some probably Britons. There would have been military clubs and organisations akin to the British Legion established at *Viroconium* concerned with the interests of these soldier-farmer/land-owners, and it is not difficult to understand that a logical step would have been the creation of a permanent army unit, into which the sons of this military gentry could have been recruited. This was

Coh. I Cornoviorum which is listed in the fourth century at Pons Aelius (*Newcastle-upon-Tyne*).[12] Hadrian, with his broad concept of military strategy and fine eye for country, had appreciated how vulnerable the province could have been to attack through the Midland Gap across the broad Shropshire Plain. It may be this factor which accounts for the presence here of old soldiers, the formation of the only known auxiliary unit from a British tribe and above all, the wealth and importance of *Viroconium*.

The villas

At present eight buildings are known which could be described as villas, and the most promising in size and quality is that at Lea Cross, first discovered in 1793, when several rooms were exposed, one of which had a mosaic with a geometric pattern.[13] The area was re-opened and extended, first by Dr. A.W.J. Houghton, and later by Mr. Geoffrey Toms.[14] The extensive disturbance has made it difficult to obtain much information about the history of the site or layout of its buildings. Three main periods have been detected, the first producing mid-second century pottery associated with good quality masonry of a building which may have been a bath-house. The foundations of these walls were used in phase 2, but the use of the building changed and to this structure was added a large barn, into which a corn-dryer had been inserted; these later periods seem to be of the third century. The area so far investigated is too small for any general conclusions and may represent parts of buildings on the edge of a large establishment. These remains are by a stream and at the bottom of a slope, and if one compares this situation with those of other villas, it seems possible that the main house and courtyard are at a higher level and yet to be located. Lea Cross may be the principal establishment of several farms along the valley of the Rea. One of these is at Cructon, 2 km. away, found during housing development in 1952-4.[15] It appeared to be a small house of only four rooms, but there may have been other adjacent buildings. Another building may exist on the south side of the brook almost 3 km. to the east at Whitley.[16]

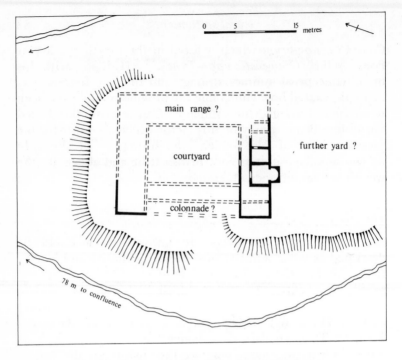

Fig. 33. Suggested plan of the villa at Yarchester

A villa which may be more substantial than the known remains indicate is Yarchester, on the slopes of Wenlock Edge almost 10 km. south-east of Wroxeter. Small-scale excavations were carried out from 1956 to 1958 by W.A. Silvester with the help of school children from Much Wenlock.[17] A range of six rooms was cleared, and one of these had a south-projecting apse with a tessellated pavement of interlaced guilloche squares and a central medallion of a 'sunflower' pattern, typical of fourth-century work.[18] This appears to be the southern range of a small courtyard villa, about 61 m. by 46 m. with buildings on the other three sides and a possible central entrance on the west. The villa was conveniently situated between two streams and the plan of the platform suggests a further yard and buildings to the south (fig. 33). The only coin recorded from the site is one of Constantius II (A.D. 337-361) and the pottery suggests third-fourth century occupation.

The building at Acton Scott, also on Wenlock Edge but

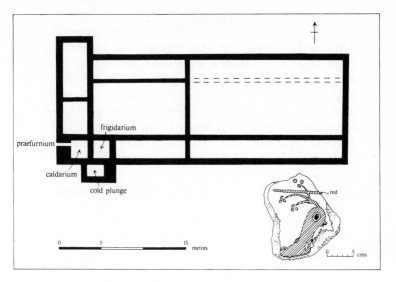

Fig. 34. Plan of a building at Acton Scott (inset: painted plaster showing a peacock?)

south of Church Stretton, is on a south-facing slope 100 m. above a stream, a typical villa situation. Found in 1817, and examined in more detail in 1844, it appears to be a rectangular building with additions at the south-west corner.[19] A lack of correspondence exists between the plans published in *Archaeologia* and *VCH* and that in the manuscript in the Bodleian, Oxford,[20] but from parallels elsewhere it is probable that the building originated as an aisled barn and was later partly converted into a dwelling house. The heated rooms in the south-west corner are presumably the remains of a small bath-house, assuming that some walls are missing, presumably having been robbed. Even so there are difficulties, since there are two pairs of flues with boiler stands, and one can only guess that there have been some drastic alterations. A possible original and revised scheme are suggested (fig. 34) which makes some sense of the remains. They do not explain, however, the room added at an angle, at the south-west corner. This had a tiled floor covered with burnt clay which had the appearance of an oven, but the position of the flue was anomalous. Only a further study of the actual remains will resolve these problems. The pieces of wall plaster found in the excavation are now in the

Shrewsbury Museum, and apart from the bordered panels there are fragments which have a more ambitious decorative scheme including one with the head of a crested bird which may have been intended as a peacock (fig. 34). This evidence and the discovery of a well-turned sandstone pillar 1 m. high indicates the presence of a house in the vicinity, which had a colonnaded verandah, and which may have been demolished when the barn-like building was converted into a dwelling. This possibility might perhaps be associated with a change of ownership, especially if farms were being amalgamated. An owner's house might no longer have been required and may have been replaced by premises more suitable for a bailiff or tenant. The site has not been touched since 1844 and earthworks in the park clearly indicate other buildings. Perhaps the oddest finds here were the five Greek coins, ranging in date from 300 to 700 B.C., and one struck by Mark Antony. They can have nothing to do with the villa and must have been lost from a collection possibly belonging to an eighteenth-century resident of the Hall.

Remains of a Roman building are recorded four miles to the north-east at Rushbury, presumably brought to the surface by the plough about 1850,[21] and traces of another have been recorded near Stanton Lacy, near Bromfield, where masonry, flue tiles, pieces of concrete flooring and pottery were dug up in 1911 during the cutting of a trench for a drain on a farm held by Mr. H. Horton.[22] In the south-west corner of the territory, about 10 km. due west of Leintwardine at Stowe near Knighton, remains of a Roman building were investigated by J.A. Morris in 1924.[23] They were found in a field called Church Field, doubtless from walls encountered earlier by the plough. A range of rectangular rooms was uncovered, including one with an apse, with the usual pieces of wall plaster, *opus signinum*, floor tiles etc. This may be part of a villa and it seems to be too far from Leintwardine to have had military connections.

In the north-eastern area there is a modest villa at Hales by the Coal Brook, a tributary of the Tern. Partly uncovered in 1928,[24] two buildings were investigated in 1966 and 1967[25] at right angles to each other, one being part of a building with a corridor and the other a bath-house, which revealed

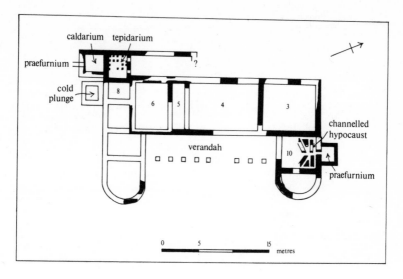

Fig. 35. Suggested plan of the villa at Engleton in its first period

considerable alterations. If these structures were built round a central courtyard, the main house was probably on the north side with a south facing aspect. The dating evidence was not in great quantity but suggests occupation from the late first into the mid-fourth centuries.

A villa which has been more thoroughly excavated is that at Engleton, overlooking the river Penk, 400 m. south of Watling Street at *Pennocrucium*. The relationship of the building to the nearby settlement may put it in a special category, possibly that of an official residence for a local customs or district officer,[26] especially in view of the important junction where the roads to Wroxeter and Chester divide, so it may not be surprising that the iron objects do not include any recognisable farm tools and there is no indication of agricultural buildings. The excavations of 1937,[27] excellent for the period, revealed a winged corridor house with baths in one corner at the rear. The plan of the Period 1 building and its suggested internal arrangements create difficulties which are not easily resolved, but an attempt has been made based on two principal assumptions (fig. 35). Firstly, the two wings at the front have projecting apses and this suggests that the southern one was similar to its pair, and therefore that the main block would have been

Fig. 36. Aerial view of an enclosure near Woolston, north of Craven Arms

symmetrical and these must be Period 1 walls to the south corner. This would also fit with the bath-house which is an extension at the west corner. There is no indication that the south wing was heated like its counterpart, which had a channelled hypocaust heated from a *praefurnium* (Room 2), but in view of the awkward planning of this wing a reorganisation is suggested. The second point is that the internal divisions of the bath-house, as given, are not possible. The *frigidarium* must have been Room 8, with its attached cold plunge, and this was the original scheme. The floor of the room labelled '*frigidarium*' was probably that of the original *caldarium*, and plate IX in the excavation report shows that its floor level was the same as that of the *tepidarium*. There are indications of the flues connecting these rooms, which were later blocked. As often happened, the *praefurnium* reached a state beyond repair and the arrangement was switched around with a new *praefurnium* and *caldarium* built at the north end. The apse of the *caldarium* is clearly an added structure. The doubling of the flue may have been the result of further alteration.

The absence of a verandah at the front in Period 1 suggests that in this period there may have been a row of column bases, subsequently buried below the later walls. Another difficult problem is Room 3, with its 'buttresses' on four sides. It is possible that they were supports for a timber floor at a later period. Among the finds were a fine crossbow brooch, a fragment of another, and a ringhead pin of a late form.

Apart from the examples discussed above there are no other villa buildings known in the Cornovian countryside, but there must be others awaiting discovery. One possible candidate is a place with the significant name of Stanchester,[28] 3 km. south-west of Wroxeter, near the point where the Roman road crosses the Cound Brook. It would have been a suitable site for a villa, but there are no recorded finds of Roman material. Another villa may yet be found near Upton Cressett, where a large quantity of pottery of the second to fourth centuries has been turned up by the plough.[29]

Peasant settlements

Aerial reconnaissance over Britain in the last four decades has been responsible for filling some of the large gaps in our knowledge of human settlement (fig. 36). Much of the lighter subsoils, and some of the heavier ones also in south-eastern Britain, are now known to have been farmed to an increasing extent through the prehistoric period and into early historic times, as is amply demonstrated in the other volumes of this series. One might expect this intensity of occupation to thin out towards the west and north. Mr. Arnold Baker has carried out many years of flying in the Avon and Severn valleys, and his results bear this out. Whereas in the Warwickshire Avon valley the evidence of agriculture and settlement forms an almost continuous band along the river terraces,[30] in the Severn these areas are detached, but nevertheless considerable. The two main concentrations are in the Bridgnorth and Wroxeter areas (fig. 37). Among the various features which

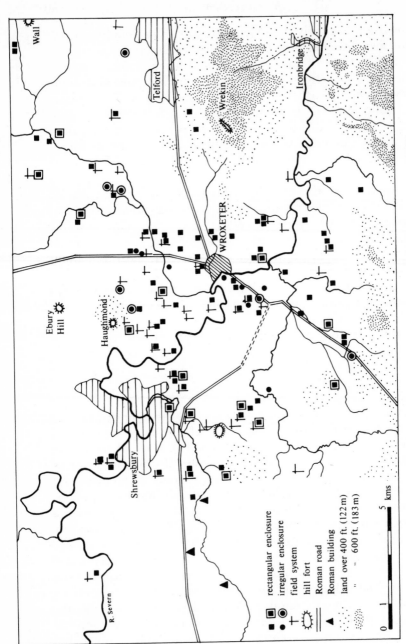

Fig. 37. Rural sites in the Severn Valley, identified from aerial photographs (based on a map by Geoffrey Toms)

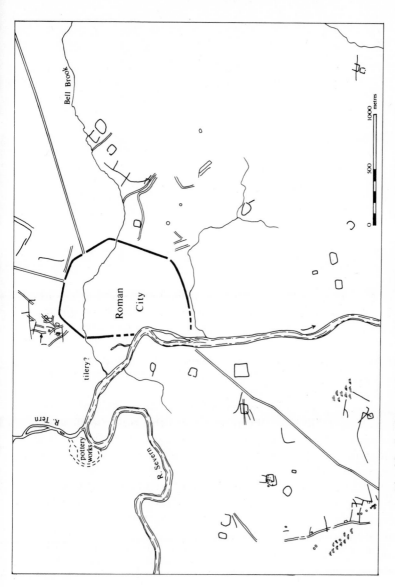

Fig. 38. Settlement in the environs of Wroxeter, identified from aerial photographs (based on a map by Geoffrey Toms)

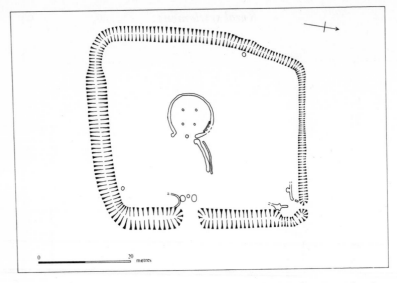

Fig. 39. The peasant settlement at Sharpstones Hill (from a plan by
W.E. Jenks)

appear as crop-marks are rectilinear enclosures and traces of
field systems (fig. 38). Mr. Jenks has already listed eleven
enclosures, mainly noted from the air, on gravel sites in the
Wroxeter area.[31] Unfortunately, it is impossible to be sure of
the dates for any of these sites, although it is a fair
assumption that most of them will be found to have been
occupied in the Roman period.

As noted earlier, where excavations have taken place, at
Sharpstones Hill and Weeping Cross, the pottery suggests
occupation in the Iron Age with continuity well into the
Roman period. The character of the sites is well illustrated by
Sharpstones Hill (fig. 39), with its enclosure ditch and its
circular hut, which was superseded by a rectangular building.
Finds from these sites indicate a low level of Romanisation
amongst the occupants. These various points are probably
true of many of these farmsteads.

The picture is at present very uncertain, but it could be
rapidly developed by a large-scale excavation of one of these
sites, and with the coming of the motorway this may happen
at any time. What is very unfortunate at present is the great
blank on the map north of Shrewsbury. Much of this area is
well suited for agriculture, and there is no reason why it

should not have been cultivated throughout all periods, and, as suggested earlier (p. 82) there may have been land development by army veterans. Traces of field systems have been recorded by Mr. Baker, however, in the Whittington area,[32] and more will undoubtedly be found with further reconnaissance.

5.

Industry and the Economy

The economic activities of the Cornovii are the most difficult of all to assess in our present state of knowledge. The most important industry of Roman Britain was agriculture, but the scanty remains discussed in the previous chapter do not encourage a high estimate of its value and extent in the tribal canton, nor indeed do they allow any worthwhile discussion of it. This chapter, therefore, will concentrate on other aspects of the economy of the *civitas*, such as pottery and tile production, and the extractive industries.

Pottery manufacture and tile kilns

The city of *Viroconium*, with its large population, would have attracted its own industries. The public buildings at Wroxeter would have utilised a vast quantity of tile, since not only were the roofs fully covered, but there were the courses of large bonding tiles in the walls, such as are still to be seen in the 'Old Work'. The bath-house absorbed many other kinds of tile for the hypocaust systems and flues. Private houses did not use this great quantity but there were enough of them in the second century to create a demand which could only be met by large tile works somewhere near the city. The site of Ismore Coppice may have been one such. The forum excavation produced three fragments of roof tiles with a maker's stamp — LCH — which, as Atkinson suggested, could have represented the initials of the three names (*tria nomina*) of a citizen.[1] Since this stamp has not been found anywhere else, however, it hints at a firm supplying the forum but no other building, and the tiles could have come from a distance, by river.

The area of a heavy tile scatter by the River Tern has been investigated on a small scale.[2] This produced many distorted tile fragments and the base of a small circular oven with a flue which had never been fired. Nearby was the floor of a timber building. The absence of any kiln structures, it was thought, might be due to the practice of firing tiles in surface clamps. The pottery sherds were all second century, and these works were probably associated with the early development of the city at the time of Hadrian. Almost certainly there would have also been extensive pottery works close to the city, supplying perhaps as much as three-quarters of all the domestic wares used there. During the military period the legion must have had its own source of supply, either a works depot or civilian contractor, since there is a very distinctive type of pottery associated with the military occupation which is found here but nowhere else. If there was a legionary works depot it might well have closed down when the legion left; a factory in civilian hands could have continued in production, although perhaps on a much reduced scale.

A large percentage of the pottery recovered from *Viroconium* is Severn Valley Ware, similar in forms and fabric to the wares found all down the valley as far south as Gloucester (fig. 40).[3] One of the centres of production of this ware was in the Malvern district where wasters have been found over a large area.[4] The slight but significant difference in fabric between the Malvern products and the pottery found at *Viroconium* indicates the strong probability that there was a major production centre near the city.

About 400 m. west of the possible tile works at Ismore Coppice, and also on the north bank of the Severn, some pottery wasters were found in 1949. A small excavation later revealed timber buildings associated with late Antonine pottery.[5] The wasters consisted of examples of fourth-century Severn Valley Ware and a group of hemispherical bowls of the same date, with a rather blunted centre flange, made in a red colour-coated ware which, in form and fabric, seems to be an imitation of the Oxfordshire wares. The

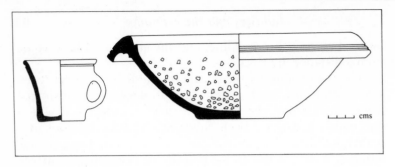

Fig. 40. A tankard of Severn Valley ware and a Rhaetian type mortarium

history and nature of the site may never be understood since the river had eroded so much, but people were clearly living here on the river bank, and possibly making pottery here in the fourth century.

The other pottery peculiar to Wroxeter is a type of *mortarium* first noticed by Bushe-Fox, and numbered in his range of types as 70, 74 and 75 (fig. 40).[6] The vessel has a very distinctive rim form; in section it is a very knobbly kind of hook with a groove on the outside and deep grooves inside to form the bead. The fabric is of a hard vitreous quality, red in colour, usually with a grey core, the result of firing at a higher temperature than usual. The surface is partly covered with a deep red slip. Bushe-Fox noted that vessels with similar characteristics have been found on military sites in Rhaetia and for this reason the type has been called Rhaetian, although it is peculiar to Wroxeter and nearby sites like Whitchurch.[7] A similar type appears to have been made at Wilderspool.[8] The period of production was in the second half of the second century, rather later than that given by Bushe-Fox.

In the Ironbridge area there are clay outcrops from the Coal Measure series and these were exploited in the eighteenth century[9] for the making of slip-wares. One of the more important of these was at Jackfield in the parish of Broseley, and these wares were produced on a large enough scale for shiploads to be sent across the Atlantic. The occurrence of refractory clays and the plentiful supply of coal led to the establishment of the famous Coalport and Caughley porcelain works, although china clay from Cornwall was much relied on. Tile and brick making was also carried out and Broseley became famous for its clay tobacco pipes. All this large-scale development, together with the coal workings and the iron foundries, have turned much of the landscape of east Shropshire into a nightmare of pits and dumps. The prospect of finding any earlier remains is indeed daunting, but it seems likely that these useful outcrops would have been exploited in the Roman period, and the ease of transport up the river to *Viroconium* is another factor in favour of this. Coal was definitely used in the Roman period but mainly for industrial purposes; the disadvantages of obnoxious fumes from its use in hypocaust heating are obvious. The find of a lathe-turned shale core at Wroxeter and two unworked lumps of shale at Lea Cross may suggest that local seams were worked for making bracelets and perhaps even as a fuel.

The stone quarries

Apart from tiles, the massive public and private buildings in *Viroconium* required large quantities of building stone. A study of the stones from the city by Cantrill[10] has led to the conclusion that almost all the rock used is sandstone. Although this varies greatly in colour, from red to yellow and grey, and also in coarseness, the paucity of fossil remains makes precise identification of the sources of the stone very difficult. Six probable sources are suggested.

1. Hoar Edge Grit, south of Wroxeter, part of the Ordovician system.
2. Lydebrook sandstone, from the Lower Carboniferous levels in Coalbrookdale and near Dawley.
3. Big Flint Rock, of the Middle Coal Measures near Ketley and Oakengates, with a quarry near Redlake (SJ 685106).
4. The Thick Rock, of the Coalport beds of the Upper Coal Measures east of Dawley.
5. Top Rock, at Madeley, from the Coalport beds.
6. The Keele Beds of the Upper Coal Measures, near Acton Burnell.

Of these possible sources the most likely to have been utilised in the Roman period are those south of Wroxeter at Hoar Edge and Acton Burnell, where there is a quarry. The former

12 INCHES

Fig. 41. A carved stone from Wroxeter showing a winged phallus

source produces very coarse buff stone with large pebbles. The carved stones forming columns, capitals, and cornices are of a finer sandstone, probably the Big Flint Rock of the Ketley area. It is perhaps significant that the stones forming the stylobate of the forum (reused, and coming from the early bath-house) contained the fossil plant *stigmaria* which is common in the Middle Coal Measures of Ketley and Oakengates.

Tufa or travertine was used in some quantity in the bath-house and there are sources of this below Wenlock limestone at Harley Brook and near Ironbridge. The roof stones are a micaceous sandstone from the lower part of the Old Red Sandstone series, probably in Corvedale where there is a quarry at Bouldon which was worked for flagstones until 1839. The stone from this source is remarkably like that of the roof slates of Wroxeter and Yarchester.[11] The great forum inscription from *Viroconium* is a fine-grained sandstone, probably from the same sequence. Other sculptured stones are also of local material (fig. 41). What is surprising is the apparent failure to use the limestone from Wenlock Edge, where there are many quarries of later ages, although this material could have been a useful source of lime for mortar.

The only carboniferous limestone in the city is found in the very white *tesserae*, almost porcelainous in character.

One other possibility of the utilisation of stone resources arises out of the name given to the military and civilian settlement at Leintwardine. The name *Bravonium*, as it appears in the Antonine Itinerary (*Iter XII*), is derived from the Celtic word for quern. This suggests that there was either a hill or rock formation here that looked like a quern, or that there were quern quarries nearby.[12] In the Upper Silurian series, the Leintwardine beds outcrop in the area and these consist of a calcareous sandstone which would have been suitable for making querns of a finer grade than could be obtained from Millstone grit, which was commonly used. Querns of this calcareous sandstone have been found at *Viroconium*.

The silver, lead and copper mines

The veins of galena which outcrop in the hills of south-west Shropshire were extensively worked in Roman times. The mineral veins occur in the Ordovician strata and the lodes were to be found on the hill slopes in an area within a distance of about six miles from the modern village of Shelve. One of the mines has been called 'Roman gravels mine'. The minerals deposited in the fissures and faults are extensive in the old rock system which has been subjected to volcanic intrusion.[13] The mineral continued to be worked in the Middle Ages and in the mid nineteenth-century it was one of the largest producers in Britain, a record output of nearly 8,000 tons being recorded in 1875. Since most of the Roman workings were in the form of open cuttings, all traces have been removed by the later operations. Although early galleries and man-made caverns have been recorded in the White Grit mine south-west of Shelve,[14] neither these, nor finds in the nineteenth century of wooden tools and candles, can be precisely dated. There is, however, positive evidence in the shape of a number of lead pigs found in the area. Five of these are recorded, all having the cast inscription *IMP HADRIANI AVG*, and in two cases a palm branch has been noted on the side of the pig.[15] The finds were all made in the

Minsterley area;[16] one is now in the British Museum, one in the Liverpool Museum, another owned by Mr. Jasper More at Linley Hall, and two have unhappily been lost. Apart from the inscriptions cast on the pigs when the lead was poured in the mould, there are often cold-struck stamps, hammered on at a later date. As all these pigs were found near the mines it can be assumed that stamps were control marks by the mine authorities, rather than by any subsequent owner or supplier. Three of the pigs were marked in this way. That at Linley Hall appears to read *MINB*, that in the British Museum *SN*, and that on a missing one is said to have read *LEG XX*. Whittick thought that this last pig was the same as that in Linley Hall and the stamp a misreading of *MINB* — ingenious but hardly plausible. These marks are often difficult to interpret. They may indicate a date, like those from Somerset (*VETP* = the consuls of A.D. 49, Veranius and Pompeius), or the initials of part of the name of a procurator in charge of the mine, as in the case of pigs from Mendip (*TI CL TRIF*),[17] or of the company operating the mine as on one from *Clausentum* (*NOVEG SOC NO*). If the reading of the Linley Hall stamp *MINB* is correct, it most likely is the *tria nomina* of a procurator *M(ARCUS) IN(. . .) B (. . .)*.

The Roman interest in these British mines was the silver, lead being merely a useful by-product. The silver content of the Shropshire ores was rather low, 2.5 oz. per ton at best, and in samples from Snailbeach it is as low as ½ oz. per ton. These figures compare unfavourably with the galena from the Mendips and the best of the Flintshire veins, where the silver content is four or five times as much. This may explain why the Shropshire mines seem to have had a short life and why the Derbyshire mines, which were similarly low in silver, were leased to a private company. The imperial control may indicate an initial hope of silver, but one also has to remember the need of lead in great quantities in the new city of *Viroconium* where the forum and private development required lead for pipes, tanks and roof gutters and flashings.

A site which could be associated with the mines is that found in the grounds of Linley Hall in 1856. The structures recorded by Wright[18] are quite extraordinary and difficult to interpret. They appear to extend over an area of about twelve

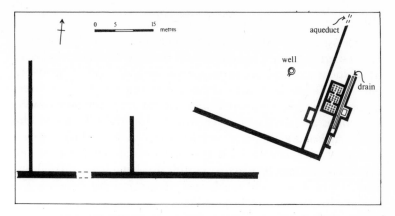

Fig. 42. Plan of the Roman buildings at Linley Hall

acres with extensive and complicated earthworks in places, but only parts of the southern end of the site were investigated. The remains consisted of two different massive structual elements at an angle to each other, such that one could hardly imagine they could be contemporary (fig. 42). The westernmost of these includes a wall, said to be almost 4 m. thick(!)[19] which seems to be a boundary wall enclosing a vast gravelled area, including the site of the present Hall. The other buildings, at an angle to this, are even more difficult to explain. There is a small block of three heated rooms, each about 3 m. square but without any sign of a *praefurnium.* On the east side is a well-built drain 'bordered by what appears to have been a channel formed of curiously constructed flue-tiles', but what this enigmatic observation really means is impossible to determine without a drawing or seeing the actual tiles. On the other side of the heated block is an aqueduct consisting of a concrete channel on a stone wall, traced 260 m. to the north to a point beyond the Hall. The aqueduct runs parallel to and by the side of the river, the West Onny, suggesting that either the river levels were too varied for a reliable and constant flow or that the head of water was the major factor. The fall of about 30 m. could have provided power also for a system of water wheels for grinding, and/or a trip-hammer for crushing, the ore. There is an open channel at the top end which is wide enough to have been a canal for narrow barges, and higher up is a by-pass and a basin. Beyond this the channel narrows to become a leat taking water from the river. The heated block of three rooms, connected with the aqueduct and drainage system, seems to be associated with some industrial process and is probably part of a larger and more elaborate arrangement. The nearest mines considered to be of Roman origin are three miles away, but there are shafts of unknown date in the hills above the Hall. Although the site would seem a fine choice as an administrative centre with the offices and residence of the *procurator*, some processing could also have been carried out here. Until more field work and excavation are done on the site all this remains very speculative.

Another metal exploited was copper, which outcrops in the Habberley area to the east and north-east of the lead mines round Shelve. There were four copper mines in the nineteenth century, but the veins are very thin and dispersed, the ores occurring as secondary minerals, chalcocite and malachite, and the yields could never have been very great. More important was the district round Llanymynech on the borders of the modern county. Ancient workings exist in the area of the Ogof in the form of pits and extensive galleries and caverns. That some of these are of Roman origin is shown by the discovery of burials and of coins and pottery of the third and fourth centuries,[20] indicating that people were living, and burying their dead, in these man-made recesses, perhaps after the early-won copper had been extracted. A hoard of thirty-three *denarii* of the late second century, found by accident in 1965 buried in a spoil heap in the 'Shaft Chamber', may, however, have been buried by a miner.[21]

Metalworking at Viroconium

The three metals produced in the tribal territory, lead, silver and copper, must have contributed something to the wealth of the tribe, although the imperial government and private companies took the major profits. It could have stimulated the manufacturers of metal articles and there is evidence from *Viroconium* to suggest bronze working. A rectangular wrought iron die (28.5 x 8.2 x 1.5 cm.) was found in the forum excavation,[22] and has designs in *intaglio* cut on both sides (fig. 43). The designs consist of rosettes, curved

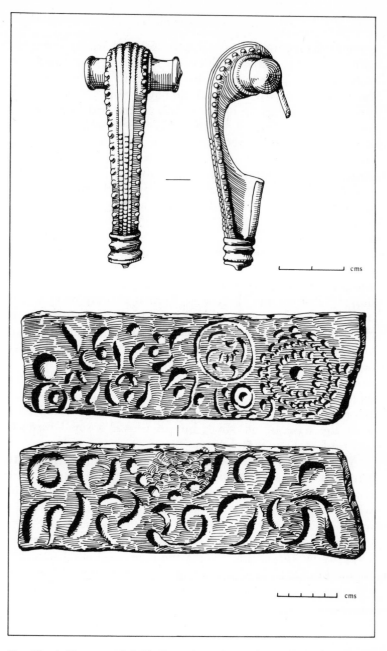

Fig. 43. A Wroxeter dolphin brooch, and two faces of an iron die for embossing bronze plates

trumpet-shaped bosses, conical bosses and round studs, all with a strong Celtic influence. The plate was used for embossing the bronze plates by hammering the designs on to them. Such embossed strips could have been used in a variety of ways, as fittings on belts, wood caskets, and furniture, or for decorating a bucket.[23] There have been several fragments of evidence from *Viroconium* which indicate various metal processes being conducted there. Five crucibles which are identified with melting and casting silver and bronze objects exhibit defects and unworked conditions clearly indicating local manufacture.[24] Another object appears to demonstrate welding iron with the use of copper,[25] quite a sophisticated technique.

Wright's discoveries in one of the rooms of the baths *insula*, fronting the main street, are more difficult to interpret. He had no doubt that it was an enameller's workshop.[26] Part of the floor was 'formed entirely of very fine sand' which he considered had been for moulds for casting. He also noticed 'a quantity of powdered granite' and if this is not a disintegrated lump from a glacial deposit, it could have been for enamelling. From his illustrations of the room it would appear that this activity was taking place when the building was in ruins, with a large column drum on its side at floor level and a capital which Wright thought could have been the base of an anvil; but there was a small furnace, pieces of coal and metal dross.

At least one type of bronze object may be traced to Wroxeter this is a particularly large and ugly dolphin brooch (fig. 43). The occurrence of this type at Wroxeter,[27] and its wider distribution pattern, establish a good case for it being made in the city.[28] Another industry which has been evidenced at *Viroconium* is glass making. Excavations in 1972 by Dr Houghton, tracing the main road in its approach to the bridge, produced evidence[29] on the edge of the road of furnaces associated with glass slag and cullet, and pottery of the late first century; but whether this is to be linked to the military or civil occupation is not certain.

6.

The Late Fourth
and Fifth Centuries

The military situation in Britain towards the end of the fourth century had steadily deteriorated. The province was under intermittent attack by sea raiders from the north, east and west, although these were sporadic and disorganised and presumably dependent on the inclinations of small groups. The defences proved adequate, and, as Sir Ian Richmond once stated,[1] it was the lack of success by the raiders which brought them into the unlikely alliance of A.D. 367, the great 'Barbarian conspiracy'. The Roman forces in Britain met with a serious defeat and the whole province was open to the raiders.[2] Count Theodosius was selected to lead a strong force including Batavi, Herculi, Jovii and Victores. Having established himself at London he sent detachments to various parts to deal with the predatory bands of looters. Like Constantius Chlorus, eighty years earlier, he may well have appreciated the special strategical significance of the site of *Viroconium* in controlling the Midland gap. There is a curious confirmation of the use of the city as a military base in the finding at various times, mainly from the site of the basilica,[3] of six *plumbatae*, a term given by Vegetius[4] to darts or small javelins with barbed points and having their shaft encased in lead (fig. 44). According to the anonymous author of *De rebus bellicis*, it was 'hurled powerfully by hand and comes among the enemy at short range' and 'is made from a length of wood fashioned like an arrow. A piece of iron is fastened accurately on to it to give it the general appearance of a hunting spear, except that the sleeve of this iron blade is somewhat longer. A short way above the sleeve prongs are

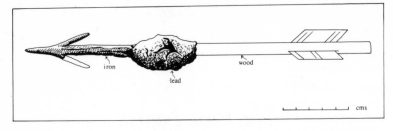

Fig. 44. A hypothetical reconstruction of a *plumbata* found at Wroxeter

affixed with lead and project like calthrops. At the other end
feathers are attached, so as to lend it speed, as much space
being left above these feathers as can be clasped by the
fingers of him who wields it'.[5] Vegetius states that each man
had five of these weapons which were held on the inside of
the shield, and that originally, under Diocletian, they were
issued only to two legions serving in Illyricum. Each received
the honorific title *Martiobarbulus* for their special skill and
dexterity in using these loaded darts, especially against
cavalry. Such was their distinguished conduct in the frontier
wars that on the accession of Maximianus in A.D. 286 they
were given the further titles Jovian and Herculean. The
implication of a further statement by Vegetius is that the
issue of these weapons were extended to other legions. In any
case, both these distinguished legions were in the force
Theodosius brought with him to Britain. The discovery of so
many of these weapons in the Wroxeter basilica may indicate
that this building was requisitioned by the army as quarters
for the legionaries and that the darts may have been lost in
the straw bedding. For the building to have been used for this
purpose it must have been standing and not in a dangerous or
ruinous condition. After Theodosius had dealt with the
raiders and secured the frontiers he turned his attention to
the cities and is credited with having 'completely restored'
them.[6] This has been interpreted by Professor Frere as the
rebuilding of the defences, with the new provision of bastions
for the housing of spring-guns.[7] As discussed above, the
original provision of defences at *Viroconium* was most
probably the work of Albinus, *c.* 196. The addition of stone
walls has been considered in many cases to have followed
during the early third century, but at Wroxeter the level at
which the wall foundations have been inserted suggests that it

must have been a long time after the original work (fig. 45). This could have been carried out when the wide ditch was dug, and a point which may favour this view is that all the excavated material went into providing a large counterscarp to increase the effective width of the ditch rather than enlarging the existing rampart, an operation which could have impeded the work of the wall builders. There has never been any positive evidence of bastions at *Viroconium*, although Mr. Arnold Baker has made a case for three possibilities[8] which still remain to be proved by excavation. This provision was made at most other cities and towns, some of them quite small, and it would have been strange if a great city like *Viroconium* had been neglected, especially as the military significance of the site seems to have been recognised. If one accepts the need of stone for walls or bastions (or both) at this period, it would have come from existing buildings and monuments. The wholesale demolition of sepulchral monuments and temples was permitted by imperial edict and proved by the discovery of fragments of these structures in the bastion foundations elsewhere. It follows that any upstanding public buildings no longer in use would have provided an excellent quarry and it is suggested that this could have been the occasion of the destruction of the enormous baths-basilica.

In 1974 excavations on the *macellum* or small market-hall in the south-west corner of the insula produced evidence of other activities at the end of the fourth century. By good fortune, the area of the colonnade along the main street had been used as a spoil dump by the nineteenth-century excavations, and they had not cleared away the upper levels as they did elsewhere. When this was stripped in 1974 a large number of post and stake holes was revealed belonging to a sequence of timber structures built into the ruins of the colonnade. At one point the line of columns had been replaced by a wattle fence. The columns, their bases and the roof had all gone, since had they collapsed, there would have been broken drums and a great strew of roof tiles. The stone gutters along the portico edge had also been taken up and a thick dark layer covered all.

From this layer came late pottery and some sixty coins,

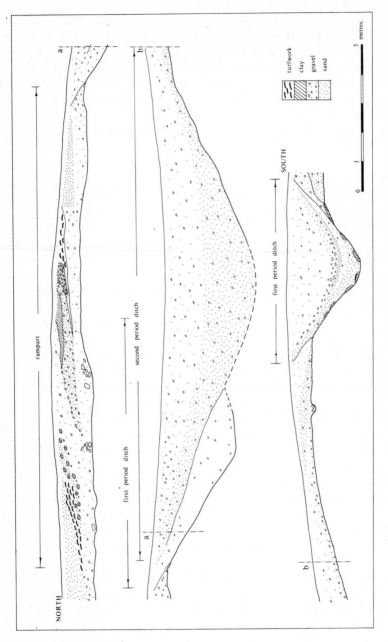

Fig. 45. Section of the defences of Wroxeter showing the two phases. The robber-trench of the wall in front of the rampart is shown stippled.

half of which belong to the House of Valentinian (A.D. 364-383), some of them distinctly worn. The inference is that there was a row of shops and booths along the street edge where the great covered colonnade had stood and that trading was brisk in the closing decades of the fourth century. The pottery at first sight looked very similar to that found by Mr. Barker in the basilica (below, p. 115) but a closer inspection shows that there are slight but significant differences. It may be possible by fabric and statistical analysis to separate the two groups and demonstrate that the one from the basilica is the later.

The work of Count Theodosius was to have a lasting effect on Britain, but the raids continued. More serious was the rapidly deteriorating situation on the frontiers elsewhere. This necessitated a steady withdrawal of troops to reinforce the field armies trying to stem the barbarian tide, or to be used in the internecine struggles for power. The *Notitia Dignitatum*, a late compilation of military units and their stations, lists no troops in Wales nor the legion at Chester. Either this is the actual situation or a section of the list has been lost. There is a hint, as Mr. C.E. Stevens pointed out long ago,[9] that the former may be the correct interpretation. Part of the *auxilia palatina* in Illyricum was a unit of Seguntienses which can only refer to men from Segontium (Caernarvon). This upgrading of British troops may, according to Mr. Stevens, have been by Magnus Maximus when he took troops from Britain to establish his position as Emperor in 383 and may also account for the disappearance of *Legio XX* from Chester.[10] Stilicho is said by the poet Claudian to have taken away from Britain, *c.* 402, 'The legion . . . that curbs the savage Irish and reads the marks tattooed upon the bodies of dying Picts . . .' a description which could have applied to all three legions. Part of the *Legio II Augusta* is at Richborough in the *Notitia* and this may have been an earlier arrangement.[11] Mr. Stevens makes a case for the XXth as the legion withdrawn in *c.* 402[12] and it certainly could not have been the XXth if it had already been taken on an occasion prior to this date.

Whatever may be the truth of this complicated sequence of events, it seems unlikely that the Welsh tribes would have been left unprotected. It was a long time since the people living in Wales had given the Roman government any serious cause for alarm. Some areas, those of the Deceangli in the north and the Silures and Demetae in the south, had had no permanent forts for generations, except the legionary base at Caerleon, and there is a growing amount of archaeological evidence of Romanisation and prosperity. These areas would have been regarded as parts of the province in need of protection. In the absence of regular Roman army units, the only other possibility was that of settling allies or coming to a favourable arrangement, if they were already there. In south-west Wales it is quite possible that a part of the territory of the Demetae had already been settled by Irish at this time. Allowing barbarian people to settle in frontier areas in return for protection had become a widespread and accepted Roman practice. It was a logical development of the earlier concept of the client kingdom and it had become quite beyond Roman resources to move them out and return the lands to their former owners; and where were the barbarians to go if they were moved?

This policy may have been developed to a further stage in northern Britain by Count Theodosius when he established four dynasties, the founders of which all had Roman names. This was a new idea, giving posts to district officers known as *praefecti* on the understanding that they remained there as petty kings and passed their title and responsibilities on to their heirs. Maximus, who had been an officer serving under Theodosius, probably set up a similar organisation in Wales using either Irish settlers or the existing Celtic tribes. The reverence with which the name of Maxen Wledic was handed down as a great folk hero of the Celtic people[13] surely indicated that he must have been seen as a liberating force in the creation of independent kingdoms under their own chiefs or kings. But it was not successful. The Irish people gradually gained command and another drastic reorganisation was needed by 430 with the transfer to North Wales of Cunedda.[14]

The closing years of the fourth century may have been anxious ones for the Cornovii. If their prosperity was dependent on the presence of the army, the departure of the units from North Wales may have been a serious loss and some businesses may have been moved elsewhere. The historical accounts which have survived give the impression of constant raids and internal turmoil, although most of the trouble was on the northern frontier and on the coasts. The Picts, Irish and Saxons were once more repulsed by the Vandal general Stilicho (395-400), but help from the central authority in Rome or Gaul became more and more uncertain. It is not surprising that the army in Britain elected a succession of leaders to take an independent command with success, since there is no hint of any great disaster. But Britain was still regarded as part of the Western Empire and for defence against the sea raiders it was essential to maintain control near the Channel ports on both sides of the water. Like Maximus, Constantine III became involved in imperial politics and was not content with his limited gains. So Britain was eventually left 'to go it alone' and this was officially recognised by the rescript of Honorius.

There is evidence of internal strife and a shift in balance of power away from the wealthy oligarchs who had dominated British civic life. Out of this arose a strong man who was able to take command of the situation and who is known to us as Vortigern, which is not a personal name but a title such as 'the high chief'. The information which has come down about this person is very confused, but one piece of evidence, the Pillar of Eliseg, implies that he was the son-in-law of Magnus Maximus and that his son Brittu was the first ruler of Powys. This places Vortigern in direct contact with the Cornovii and it is necessary to study the situation more closely.

The task confronting Vortigern about 425 when he gained, or was placed in, power, was the unification of Britain and the consolidation of the frontiers. His efforts over the following twenty-five years were highly successful. He must have had the full support of the army but only grudging acknowledgement from the civil leaders, and from his widespread popularity Vortigern clearly had the sympathy of the peasants. This suggests that he may have taken part in the civil strife which removed some of the powerful notables whose harsh and tyrannical behaviour may have been the initial cause of the trouble.

Once in command, Vortigern set about the difficult task of
frontier control. The Picts and Saxons were still a menace on
the east coast. The most vulnerable point was the Thames
Estuary, giving direct access to London. Saxon federates had
already been established in East Anglia and Essex, but by
now it is doubtful if the British fleet was still active or the
Saxon Shore forts all manned. The action Vortigern took in
428, for which he received such violent condemnation later,
was to try to replace the fleet, and the only available
warships were those of the Saxons. This is why he gave the
brothers Horsa and Hengest the Isle of Thanet, on condition
they kept watch on the Thames estuary and drove off
invaders. The following year it was necessary to restore order
in north Wales. The native rulers had not been strong enough
to resist the Irish, who now combined with the Picts in an
attempt to gain control of the Midland gap which would have
given them access to the Midlands and the south. This
combined attack took place at Easter and Vortigern sought
the aid of the great soldier, Bishop Germanus of Auxerre,
who was visiting Britain to deal with the Pelagian heresy.

There is in his biography a graphic and detailed account of
the campaign which culminated in a valley surrounded by
high hills and the famous 'Alleluia' victory. The enemy fled,
many drowning in the river as they were forced to cross it.
This is most likely to have been in Wales, and there are early
traditions of Germanus in the Vale of Llangollen where the
Dee can still be a treacherous river when swollen by heavy
rains. This victory marked a change on frontier policy which
Vortigern was now strong enough to initiate. The native kings
had failed and had to be replaced. This is the time which best
fits the advent of Cunedda. He was the grandson of Patern
Pesrat, Paternus of the Red Robe, a man whose cloak was the
mark of rank and authority. He has been considered as one of
the Roman officers given kingdoms beyond the Wall by
Theodosius in 380. Paternus became the ruler of the Votadini
on the north-east coast. If he was then in his prime, Cunedda,
his grandson, would have been about the right age for a
similar transfer some fifty years later. He left behind his
kinsmen to continue their frontier responsibilities, while he,
with eight sons and warriors, set about the clearance of the

Irish settlers in Wales, with great slaughter, according to the fragment recorded by Nennius. The recovery could not have been swift, but was probably planned year by year. If the Roman roads and forts were used it seems likely, as John Morris suggests,[15] that Cunedda's main base, at least at the outset, was Chester; but archaeological evidence to support this historical patchwork is still very thin. Gradually, Cunedda and his sons gained control of most of Wales, but the boundaries of the main kingdom remained the rivers Dee and Teifi.

If, as has been thought, the name is derived from the Roman '*Pagenses*', 'the people of the countryside', the kingdom of Powys may have been one of the creations of Maximus, since it lies to the west of the Cornovii in the hill country under Roman military control. The Pillar of Eliseg gives the origin of the dynasty to Brittu, a son of Vortigern. In the life of St. Germanus a wicked king was deposed and replaced by a man named as Catal 'from whose seed Powys is still ruled'. The confusion may have arisen through the change in the ruler having been carried out under the authority of Vortigern, the original dynasty set up by Maximus having proved too tyrranical.

The problem of the Irish raids and settlement on the west coast was eventually solved by St. Patrick's vigorous mission and sealed by the marriage of a daughter of Vortigern to a son of the High King. This may have led to a long period of peace for the Cornovii, although the inhabitants of Wroxeter were now living in a decaying city. The breakdown of the money economy had led to an intricate system of payment and barter in goods and services. It would have been difficult, unless a powerful citizen could command a labour force, to carry out any building or repair work, and this led, inevitably and gradually, to a diminution of technical skill and experience. Buildings were patched and propped up, and it is surprising how long substantial structures can survive under these conditions. The main problem may have been that of the supply of materials, especially tiles, which had ceased being manufactured much earlier, about the middle of the fourth century. Consequently, they became much sought after, and buildings containing them were often gutted. The heated rooms of the bath-house at Wroxeter had the thick concrete floors smashed and the supporting tiles underneath prised out. Even more surprising is the enormous labour of burrowing along the drains in order to remove all the tile linings. The people who did this must have known exactly where the drains were, and probably carried out this work when the system was still visible. The trenches and holes they left were used as rubbish tips, and the great quantity of animal bones is clear evidence of the presence of a thriving community.

The excavations at Wroxeter, which have been extensive since the middle of the last century, have not produced a single artefact that can be dated from the fifth to the seventh century, except for one which was turned up by the plough in 1967. It was found on the outer edge of the counterscarp of the defences in the north-eastern area of the city,[16] and is a stone which has been recut several times. It finally became the tombstone with the inscription:—

CUNORIX
MACUS MA
QVI COLINE

The last line is not entirely certain, owing to damage by the ploughshare, but the name of the man commemorated is Celtic: the first part, Cuno, means a hound or a mighty one, and the second part is Rix, a king. The name itself, and the fact that he has a tombstone, mark him out as a leader or ruler. The second line begins Macus, which means 'son of', a prefix to become widely used later after the Irish migration into Scotland. The name of the father is given, 'Son of the Holly'. The stone can be dated on linguistic grounds and it is the carefully considered opinion of Professor K.H. Jackson[17] that it belongs to the second half of the fifth century, or possibly a little later. Another conclusion is that Cunorix was an Irishman and not a Briton. Thus we have an important man from Ireland buried at Wroxeter at some time in the fifth century. An obvious inference is that he was a mercenary soldier employed by the citizens for protection; could he have been placed there as part of Vortigern's frontier arrangements of *c.* A.D. 430? Without further evidence this can only be regarded as a speculation.

While there are no other datable objects, the archaeological evidence recovered by Mr. Philip Barker on the site of the basilica is strongly suggestive of continuity from the fourth century.[18] These discoveries have only been made possible by the excavation techniques used. Work began in 1966 in the north-east corner of the *insula* to test the area to see if it was possible for it to be used as a visitors' car park. When the plough soil was stripped off a sequence of buildings of slight construction was revealed. The floors were clearly discernible, but the wattle and daub walls only yielded to very careful work. This discovery was so unexpected in the centre of a great Roman city that it was decided, in full agreement with the Department of the Environment, to continue the excavation to the west. This led to the total clearance of the plough-soil from the site of the basilica, or exercise hall, but everything else was left intact, a lengthy process not completed until 1973. As one might expect, the site was found to be criss-crossed by earlier excavators' trenches and some areas cleared to the basilica floor, but sufficient remained of the latest undisturbed levels to reveal an astounding pattern of rectangular platforms constructed of carefully selected rubble. This could easily have been dismissed as a random scatter, the results of stone robbing and land clearance, had it been seen in trenches or small areas. It was the total horizontal view which produced a convincing pattern of rectangles (fig. 46), but the proof that this is the ground plan of a large and elaborate building is in the entrance. This consisted of an unfinished Roman capital and a re-used column, carefully placed at 3.40 m. centres. The western one is still in its original position but the other has been tipped at an angle by the plough. These stones were clearly the pads for the timber posts of an entrance of some pretension, nor is this the only evidence of this type of structure. Along the south aisle was a series of roughly rectangular platforms, evidently for buildings or lean-to's against the upstanding south wall of the basilica. The most difficult archaeological problem is that of the Roman street running east-west along the north side of the basilica. For a length of 65 m. almost symmetrical to the main platform, the hard packed gravel of nine successive streets had been

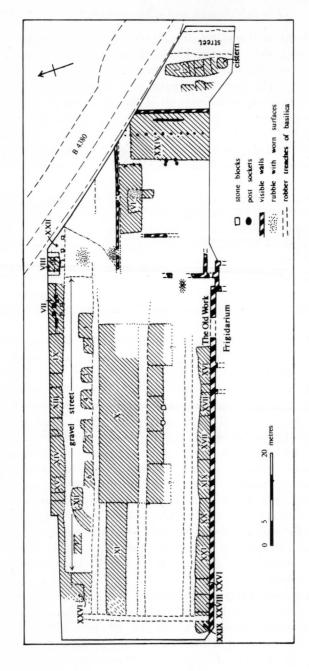

Fig. 46. The Wroxeter basilica site: plan of rubble platforms for timber structures and other buildings (from a plan by P. Barker)

removed and replaced by a sandy silt which had the appearance of being sieved. Platforms were faintly visible on its surface, presumably those of buildings against the north side of the main platform. The reason for this strange construction is not yet apparent, but the whole complex can be seen as a major building project covering much of the site of the basilica.

That such a series of structures could only have been conceived and occupied by a person of outstanding power and influence must be conceded. The character of the buildings is an equally important aspect, for there are no post holes or construction trenches, and the clear inference is that the buildings were timber-framed. This kind of construction was not new to Roman Britain and there were probably far more buildings of this type than is fully realised. The stone sills usually found in private houses in both town and country suggest timber-framed structures; the stone walls merely lift them above ground level to where the timbers were less likely to suffer from wet or dry rot. The plan of the principle building (X) is of a Romano-British type, the winged corridor house with a central entrance. What is astonishing is that this should be wholly of timber when there was so much stone available from the ruined public buildings all around; or were they all occupied as tenements? It is not, however, a typical town house plan, but of a type normally known only from the countryside, where they are associated with a large courtyard, surrounded by ancilliary buildings. These latter structures are here, but squeezed into the basilica rectangle. Thus we have a powerful character, building himself a kind of country mansion in the middle of the city, surrounded with small buildings, which are either stables or, in view of their apparent numbers, houses for his retainers. The construction method is no longer in stone but entirely in timber, on carefully laid rubble platforms to secure adequate drainage. Furthermore, it has none of the appurtenances of the wealthy private houses, as there are no centrally heated rooms and above all no bath-suite. Here there is not merely a break, but a wide gap between the sophisticated Roman way of life and that of the barbarian. A picture begins to emerge of a shadowy world retaining some elements of the past which are not appropriate to the situation, but ideas which are new and forward looking. A vigorous force is in command, and from whatever source it came, there was a wish to have some semblance of the classical past from which authority could have been tenuously extended.

But when did this take place? The relationship of these structures to the basilica is curious. The great aisled hall was completely demolished in late Roman times, as postulated above, in all probability to provide stone for the building of the defensive wall around the city under Count Theodosius, c. 380. The south aisle wall was left standing and the outer walls were, at this stage, only taken down to ground level. While the great timber building platform was spread over the robber trench of the north aisle wall, there are robber trenches cut through it along the stylobate walls which supported the main columns of the nave; the stone gutters have also been robbed out along the south side of the street. Thus there are at least two stages of robbing, one before the erection and occupation of the great timber building and one after. It is not possible to determine the dates of this activity until the trenches are completely excavated and all the artefacts in them fully examined, but the second stage could be very late indeed. There are accounts of walls and column bases being removed for building boundary walls in the nineteenth century,[19] but Mr. Barker has posed an interesting question — if these walls were so completely buried, how would anyone know they were there? This may have been due to chance discovery in digging or ploughing at any period. None of this, however, helps in the dating of the large timber structures; this must await further excavation. Already it is clear that there are many floor levels over the original basilica floor and below the platforms, but this may merely represent the patching of over two hundred years, except that some of them do not appear to be continuous or the kind of floors suitable for a great public building. The possibility remains of a period of time elapsing before the destruction of the basilica and the building of the platforms, when the great hall may have been divided up and put to other uses. The differential weathering of the floors of the nave and aisles show that during this period there was a time when the roof of the nave was removed but the aisles remained protected.

This archaeological evidence must take us, by inference, well into the fifth century, and Cunorix presents firm ground for Wroxeter being still occupied and in British hands until the end of the century. This is the time of Arthur, when it becomes very difficult to separate fact from myth and legend. That there was a great British leader who stopped further Saxon advance westwards and secured an interval of peace seems fairly certain. If the victory of Mount Badon was *c.* 500 this would mean that *Viroconium* survived into the sixth century.

The most crucial event for the Midlands in the sixth century was the defeat of the British in 571 by Cuthwulf, somewhere near Bedford. This opened the way for Saxon expansion to the west, and six years later another serious blow was struck at Dyrham, near Bath, which must have led to the collapse of the old Roman *civitas* of the Dobunni. There is as yet no evidence of Saxon settlement in the Cotswolds as early as this, although there is a suggestion of a further Saxon victory in the lower Severn in 584. But there are also traditions of the English failing to gain any foothold in the border lands of south Wales. News of these events must have been disturbing to the Cornovii, but they were safe for the present under the strong protective rule of Urien of Reged, whose fame is recorded by his bard Taliesin. The battleground of the late sixth century was the north-west, where Urien and his British and Irish allies almost succeeded in crushing the power of the English until the great king was killed by treachery. The lack of unity among the British leaders led to their undoing and the English rose powerfully to the challenge. Their victory at Catterick in 598 established their control over the Pennines, and the northern tribes were nearly defeated in 603. Aethelferth was well enough established by 614 to turn towards north Wales and at the battle of Chester he defeated the combined forces of Gwynedd and Powys which by now presumably included all or most of the territory of the Cornovii. It was a victory for the pagans too, and a thousand monks from Bangor-on-Dee are recorded as slain; as Aethelferth logically concluded, 'if they invoke their God against us, they fought against us even if they bear no arms'.

The effect of this English success must have been similar to that of Dyrham; the country lay open for invasion and pillage. The situation at Wroxeter was now finally untenable; with many of the best of the fighting men slain at Chester, the inhabitants would now have been well stretched to man the great circuit of the city defences. It was probably now or a little later that Edwin, the successor of Aethelferth, was able to march uninterrupted into north Wales. If they had not moved before, this would have been the occasion for the citizens to transfer themselves and their belongings to a place of greater safety. There is no evidence of the place they selected, but the possibilities which immediately commend themselves are the sites of Shrewsbury, or The Berth, near Baschurch or one of the great Iron Age hill-forts. The former is virtually a rocky island surrounded by river and marsh and for complete protection only a short length of ditch and bank or stockade was needed. The Berth is a fortified island in a marsh, ideal as a refuge. A small-scale excavation at the latter has revealed Iron Age occupation and the excavator, Mr. P.S. Gelling, gives a hint of post-Roman possibilities.[20] Since Wroxeter has produced no artefacts dated between 400 and 800 it is not likely that they will be found on either of these sites, but excavations might reveal buildings which could be placed in this context. The Berth offers much greater possibilities for further discoveries than Shrewsbury, where mediaeval and modern development have already removed most of the early levels.[21]

Viroconium was never entirely abandoned; there would have been those who had little to lose and who depended on the land for their sustenance and livelihood. There is sufficient evidence for a period when the centre of the city became the cemetery of a nearby community. The skeletons found by Wright in the basement of a hypocaust of the baths are difficult to explain. The discovery, of two females and an old man, was made in the *tepidarium* of the added bath-suite on the west side of the main block. Near the old man was the remains of a small wooden box with a heap of

132 coins, the latest of which was one of Valens. To a nineteenth-century antiquary this was graphic evidence. These poor folk, crawling for safety into the hypocaust system with their life savings, had been suffocated by the building being burnt over their heads. More recent excavation has, however, produced no indication anywhere of a final holocaust. It is more likely that these are burials made in the ruined building after the floors had been broken for the extraction of tiles; the coins are probably a small hoard deposited at an earlier date. There are other burials which have been recorded by Bushe-Fox,[22] one of which had been cut into a building. Fragments of human skeletons were also found in disturbed soil and in 1973, a part of a lower jaw was found in the colonnade in front of the market hall. Atkinson recovered similar evidence from the forum,[23] including a complete skeleton with a displaced skull found lying on the edge of the main street with 'a thin film of earth' separating it from the latest street. Atkinson suggests that this was a corpse left lying at the edge of the street, but the careful way in which the skull has been detached and placed at the feet[24] shows that this had been a definite burial. The implication of this is that the ground level at this period was at least two feet above the latest street level. There is, then, a considerable amount of evidence to suggest that the centre of the city became a cemetery. A few casual burials might be considered the result of a breakdown of the Roman practice which insisted on burials outside the walls of a town, but when found undisturbed, it is clear that all these skeletons have been placed in properly organised burials, some even in an east-west axis. The conclusion is that at this period the nucleus of the community was no longer here but nearby, perhaps on the site of the Wroxeter village.

The threat of the powerful Anglian dynasts of Northumbria forced a strange alliance between the adjacent peoples of Christian Powys and pagan Mercia. Penda had strengthened his position by a pact with Cadwallon of Gwynedd which led to the defeat of Edwin on Hatfield Chase in 632 and the destruction of the King of Deira and his army the following year. It looked as if the Britons were poised once more to break the power of the English in the north-east, but it was not to be. Oswald, now King of Deira, caught Cadwallon in a chance encounter near Hexham and killed him.[25] He was now able to unite his kingdom with Bernicia, consolidate his position and develop as a great king, honoured later as a saint.

It was not until 641 that Oswald felt himself strong enough to lead his army south to face the combined forces of Penda and Powys, but he suffered defeat and death at the battle of Maserfelth, later to be named Oswestry after him. This made Penda the most powerful king in Britain and, as his close allies, the people of Powys were now safe and secure. The friendly relationship with the Mercians allowed for gradual penetration and English settlement followed in east Shropshire. One of the sons of Penda was Merewalh, who is recorded as king of the Magonsaeta,[26] an area which appears to stretch from the Wye to the Wrekin and comprised much of east Herefordshire and south-east Shropshire. Among his possessions was the land purchased from him for the founding of a convent at Much Wenlock in 680,[27] of which his daughter Mildburg eventually became abbess. The life of St. Mildburg relates how her father was baptised in 660, so it is clear that the kingdom had become established with the approval of the British some time after alliance with Penda and that English settlement in this area was taking place gradually throughout the following years. In 654 the situation changed again when Penda fell before Oswin the brother of Oswald, somewhere near Leeds. This destroyed the great Mercian kingdom but also aroused old and almost forgotten rivalries, and it is against this background that one must assess the next event in the story.

This is recorded by one of the Powys poems of Llywarch Hen, and tells of the deeds of the hero Cynddylan, son of Cyndrwyn, who lived in his great hall at Pengwern in the white town by the woods. Many scholars, including Dr. John Morris, have identified this place as the Roman city of *Viroconium* from the inference that the description would have been that of a stone-built town. The poem does not lack place-names but the difficulty is in deciding where the topographical details are meaningful and where poetic imagery is involved. For example, Heledd, the sister of

Cynddylan, is said to 'be gazing at or from Dinlleu Vreconn'; if this is identified as the Wrekin, which is not certain,[28] it places Pengwern on top of, or within sight of, this dominant peak.[29]

The Wrekin is not a very hospitable place for a residence, nor does it fit the other details in the poem. The name Pengwern means 'the head of the alder grove' or 'alder-hill', and alder is a shrub normally found in marsh or swampy conditions, which seems to exclude the rocky Wrekin whose scant subsoil only supports bracken. A more obvious choice would be Shrewsbury or The Berth. The historical tradition which has identified the former with this name stems from Geraldus Cambrensis (*c.* 1200), a late and not always reliable source. Also, Shrewsbury had its own earlier Welsh name (Amwythig). A strong factor in favour of The Berth is that it is only a mile from Baschurch, which must be Eglwysau Basa[30] to which the body of Cynddylan was carried. The Powys poem seems to imply that Cynddylan was protecting his frontier, given as the Tren (=Tern) which is west of Wroxeter. On the other hand, he is also said to live 'between Tren and Trodwydd', or Tern and Roden, a large area in which is situated the finest of all Shropshire hill-forts, Bury Walls, with swampy ground to the south. No satisfactory conclusion to this problem can be offered but one day, perhaps, the great hall of Cynddylan will be found by excavation, for this is the only way in which the evidence can now be produced.

The epic in which the hero was so revered glorifies the raid on Lichfield, *c.* 655. When Penda was killed in 654, he was succeeded by his son, Peada, who was baptised and founded a monastery at Lichfield. But Peada was a dependant of Oswy of Northumbria, and his conversion had been by Finan of Lindisfarne. This could be seen as an opportunity for the Britons to revenge themselves against the Northumbrians, for the slaughter of the monks of Bangor at Chester.[31] But apart from 'the book-clutching monks who fell in their bloody enclosure' there were 'the fifteen hundred cattle and five herds of swine'. It was this cattle raid, later magnified into a great heroic tale by the bards, which may well have persuaded the Mercians, once they had thrown off their subservience to Northumbria, to deal firmly with the British maurauders by gaining control of the Severn, since by 660 the river had become the boundary. This is the date of the so-called Tribal Hidage, which records the people of Wroxeter as the Wrocensaetna and so is, presumably, a census made soon after the annexation. It is noteworthy that the place or its people was considered important enough to give its name to the area, but whether it is derived from *Viroconium* or the Wrekin is not certain. This was also the time of the Synod of Whitby in 663, when the Celtic church bowed to the power of Rome and St. Peter. Places were soon chosen for services and sanctified with the erection of a cross to be followed by the building of a church. Gradually the local inhabitants were persuaded to forsake their traditional burial areas in favour of the holy ground around the church. The site of the building dedicated to St. Andrew at Wroxeter is within the walled area of the Roman City, and it would be interesting to know what lies below it. The nave is built entirely of massive stones taken from the Roman city and is considered to be of Saxon type, earlier than the tenth century.[32] Built into the upper courses of the south wall is a piece of a cross shaft with panels of interlace decoration, typical of Mercian work of the ninth century.[33] If a church had been established by this period, the burials in the centre of the Roman city, mentioned earlier, must belong to the two centuries between its desertion and the start of the practice of churchyard interments.

Notes and references

References to British journals use the abbreviations recommended by the Council for British Archaeology, which are those of the American Standards Association (list Z39, 5-1963, revised 1966). Other abbreviations used are:

BM   British Museum
CAM   *Cambridge Ancient History* (Cambridge 1936)
CBA   Council of British Archaeology
CIL   *Corpus Inscriptionum Latinarum*
NMR   National Monuments Record
RCHM Royal Commission on Historical Monuments
RIB   R.G. Collingwood and R.P. Wright *Roman Inscriptions of Britain* i (Oxford 1965)
VCH   *Victoria County History*

1. TRIBAL TERRITORY AND THE PRE-ROMAN IRON AGE

 1. Dury *1959*, 205-7.
 2. Chitty *1927a*.
 3. Chitty *1927b*.
 4. Chitty *1963*.
 5. Stanford *1972a*, 32-3.
 6. Before this it was a tributary of the Trent and the Ironbridge gorge was created by the pressure of the meltwaters of Lake Buildwas (Dury *1959*, figs. 100 and 101).
 7. Barker *1970*, 10-19.
 8. Chitty *1963*.
 9. Chitty *1953*, 139-40.
10. It was noticed by Dr. A.W.J. Houghton when houses were being constructed in 1958, in what used to be called Meole Lane, but no traces were found to the east of this point. *Shrops. News Letter* iii (1958).
11. Peacock *1969*.
12. Stanford *1972b*.

13. Hawkes *1959*, ·15.
14. Stanford *1971*, 121.
15. Spurgeon *1972*.
16. Stanford *1971*.
17. Jarrett and Mann *1968*, 165; a case can be made for two tribes in North Wales with very similar names, the Decanti, a scribal gloss on Decangi (*Annals*, xii, 32), and the Deceangli of Flintshire known from the stamps on lead pigs.
18. Stanford *1972b*, fig. 3.
19. O'Neil *1934*.
20. Kenyon *1943*.
21. Dr. Stanford considers, from the spacing of the group, that the four posts, 3 m. apart, are the corners of small huts (*Shrops. News Letter* xliv (1973), 31-2; see also Stanford *1971*).
22. Gelling *1959* and *1964*.
23. Gelling and Peacock *1968*.
24. O'Neil *1937*, 86.
25. Musson *1972*.
26. As at Croft Ambrey, Stanford *1974*.
27. Varley *1950*.
28. Gelling and Stanford *1967*; Stanford *1974*, 210-14.
29. Crawford *1954*.
30. I am grateful to Mrs. Joan Miller for giving me information about her field work; see also Stanford *1974*, 231-3.
31. *W. Midlands Annual Archaeol. News Letter* ix (1966), 13-14; x (1967), 21-3; *Avon and Severn Valleys Research Project* iii (1966).
32. *W. Midlands Archaeol. News Sheet* xi (1968), 7-8 and 15; xii (1969), 17-18.
33. *Shrops. News Letter*, xli (1970), 9-11 with plan.
34. Rivet *1970*. The form Viroconiorum suggests, as Mr. Rivet has indicated (Rivet *1966*, fn. 24), that the scribe conflated Viroconium and Cornoviorum.
35. Richmond and Crawford *1949*, 47.
36. Jackson *1970*, 81.
37. *ibid.*; see also Jackson *1953*, 601.
38. *supra* fn. 34.
39. Ross *1967*, 143.
40. Thomas *1963*, 40.
41. Segontiaci, Ancalites, Bibroci and Cassi; *Gallic Wars*, v.21.
42. *J. Roman Stud.* lv (1965), 224.
43. *J. Roman Stud.* lvi (1966), 223.
44. I am most grateful to Mr. John Mann for his help in clarifying the subject for me and suggesting appropriate references.
45. It is unfortunate that of the only British inscription which could be helpful (*RIB*, 1948 from Chester-le-Street, dated to A.D. 216), only half has survived, see also Mócsy *1967*.
46. MacMullen *1963* gives examples from Egypt; another comes from Scaptopara, a small place in Thrace where troops went to enjoy the

hot-springs and helped themselves to food and entertainment, which caused the outraged villagers to petition the Emperor Gordian (*CIL*, iii, 12336).

47. Lewis and Reinhold *1955*, ii, 515-17.
48. *Annals* xi, 19.
49. As possibly with the Carvetii. The evidence comes from an altar from Brougham (*J. Roman Stud.* iv (1965), 224, No. 11) dated to A.D. 260 and a tombstone from Old Penrith (*RIB*, 933) of Flavius Martius, a senator and *questorius* of the tribe.
50. Stanford *1968*.
51. Walker *1967*.
52. *VCH Staffs.*, i (1908), 190; *Antiq. J.* xiv (1934), 183; *Britannia* ii (1971), 259.
53. Hartley *1952* and *1964*.
54. *Annals*, xiii, 54-5.
55. The northern boundary of early mediaeval Powys was at Pulford, three miles north of Holt, and Dr. Radford has suggested that this may reflect the original Cornovian limit to the north. (*Antiquity* xxxii (1958), 19-24). It has been suggested that the original boundaries of Powys were those of the Cornovii (Chadwick *1954*, 47).
56. See fn. 48 above.
57. This suggestion is developed from an idea of Professor A.L.F. Rivet (Rivet *1966*, 109).

2. HISTORY: A.D. 43-367

1. *CIL* vi, 920 '. . . *reges Brit[annorum] XI d[evictos . . .*' on the triumphal arch built in A.D. 52.
2. *Annals* xii; for a study of the evidence see Webster *1960*, *1970* and *1973*.
3. This is an interpretation based on the malicious comment of Dio (lxii, 2, 1) but most scholars would prefer a date nearer to 60. However, by the time news reached Rome of the full extent of the revolt it would have been too late to have called in any loans.
4. Webster and Dudley *1973*, fig. 6; St Joseph *1973*, 234.
5. St Joseph *1973*, 234-5 and pl. xvii, 1.
6. St Joseph *1953a*, 54; *1961*, 125; *1965*, 85.
7. *Trans. Birmingham Archaeol. Soc.* lxxix (1964), 117-120; Scott *1973*.
8. Gould *1964* and *1968*. There is also a group of marching camps west of Wall, St Joseph *1973*, 233.
9. St Joseph *1965*, 76-7; *1973*, 233.
10. St Joseph *1963*, 84; Webster *1964b*.
11. St Joseph *1969*, 105; *1973*, 233-234 and fig. 18.
12. St Joseph *1961*, 125; *1965*, 85; *1973*, 235.
13. St Joseph *1953*, 85; *1958*, 95; *Trans. Shrops. Archaeol. Soc.* lvii (1966), 197.

14. Stanford *1968*.
15. Jarrett *1969*, 116-18; *Britannia* i (1970), 273; ii (1971), 246-7; iii (1972), 302; iv (1973), 272.
16. Webster and Dudley *1973*, 146-58.
17. Birley *1953*, 1-9; *Epigraphische Studien* iv (1967), 65.
18. Dudley and Webster *1962*.
19. *RIB* 291. This stone is said to have been recovered near the blacksmith's shop which is just to the north of the central *insulae* of the later Roman city. It was presumably re-used in some later building, but it does raise the question of the whereabouts of the cemetery of the auxiliary fort. Bushe-Fox found a cremation burial with a melon bead in the lowest level of site III in 1912 (Bushe-Fox *1913*) which could have been on the main north-south road. There is another case at Chester of early cremations being found below a legionary fortress (Richmond and Webster *1950*, 18). It was a serious offence under Roman law to disturb the remains, but what would have happened to any tombstone or monument on ground selected for the erection of a legionary fortress?
20. *RIB* 292.
21. *RIB* 294.
22. *RIB* 296.
23. *RIB* 293.
24. St Joseph *1955*, 88 and pl. xix.
25. Jones *1969*.
26. Hurst *1972*, 39-40.
27. Dr. A. Birley has suggested to me that he may have come over from Germany with replacements for *IX Hisp.* in A.D. 60.
28. *Britannia* i (*1970*), 182, fn. 19; Cunliffe *1973*, 26-27, *RIB* 91.
29. *Agricola* 7 and 8.
30. Wheeler *1954*.
31. Richmond and Ogilvie *1967*, 75; see also a plan of Inchtuthil, fig. 9.
32. FORTUNAE AUGUSTI type of Domitian, the same issue which provides the dates of the demolition at Inchtuthil (Richmond and Oglivie *1967*)
33. *RCHM Eburacum* (1962) xxxiv-xxxix. The *canabae* normally tend to develop near the main gates of the fortress and spread from these points as at Aquincum and Briegetio (Mócsy *1953*, Abb. 1 and 2).
34. I owe this interesting suggestion to Mr. B.R. Hartley.
35. Houghton *1973*.
36. As did York by the early third century.
37. The evidence for *canabae* at Chester is not extensive, since there has been so much post-Roman disturbance (Thompson *1959*, 34-36).
38. The foundation of Gloucester was under Nerva in A.D. 96, but one wonders if this dedication was changed after Domitian received the

damnatio. It would have been embarrassing for the two *coloniae* to have paid regular homage to the discredited Emperor, having also the permanent erasure present on all the inscriptions; a suggestion made to me by Mr. J. Wacher.

39. Atkinson *1942*, 114.
40. Information kindly supplied by the excavator, Mr. Dennis Petch.
41. *Cathedral Close Excavations*, Exeter Museum Pub. No. 67; *Current Archaeol.* xxxix (1973), 102-10.
42. Forster and Knowles *1915*, 250-4; the evidence is summarised by Jarrett and Mann, *1970*, 181. It is not certain if this hoard was found inside the fort of this period.
43. Curle *1911*.
44. Richmond *1950*, 26.
45. Hartley *1972*, 15.
46. The evidence comes from inscriptions from gateways at Caerleon, A.D. 100 (*RIB* 330); Chester, A.D. 102-17 (*RIB* 464); and York, A.D. 107-8 (*RIB* 665). The implication here is that work started at Caerleon but the campaign caused a delay in the implementing of the new policy of at least seven years at Chester and York.
47. Well 1; Atkinson *1942*, 114.
48. Atkinson *1942*, 20-3, coin list (p. 309) of the eight decipherable coins of Domitian, seven are A.D. 86-7 and only one later, of A.D. 95.
49. Kenyon *1940*, 178 and pl. lxviii; although the early defences sectioned on the east side may have been those of the legionary fortress.
50. Baker *1971*, 204-8 and fig. 39.
51. Corder *1955*, 24. This theory has never been seriously challenged although modifications have been suggested (Wacher *1964*).
52. One of these was found at Moretonsay near Longford (*VCH Shrops. i*, 276) and another at Hordley Grange, near Ellesmere (Webster *1959*).
53. Webster *1971*.
54. This includes work at *Uxacona* in 1973, for information about which I am indebted to the excavator Mr. David Browne (*W. Midlands Archaeol. News Sheet* xvi, 1973, 20-1).
55. This has been shown by excavation at both Wall (Gould *1964*, 4) and Manduessedum (Mahany *1971*).
56. It was the substantial length of defence wall at Letocetum which gave its name to the modern village.
57. Atkinson *1942*, 108-13.
58. Wright *1872*, 121.
59. *Ammianus* xiv, 5, 6.
60. *ibid.*, xx, 1, 1.

3. COMMUNICATIONS AND URBAN SETTLEMENT

1. *Agricola* 19.
2. Meeson *1966*.
3. Gould *1968;* St. Joseph *1973*.
4. St. Joseph *1965*.
5. St. Joseph *1953*; Webster *1964b*.
6. St. Joseph *1969*, 105; *1973*, fig. 18.
7. Appearing in the Antonine Itinerary as *Iter* II and designated by Kubitschek as a *hauptlinie* ('Itinerarien' in Pauly-Wissowa), Rivet *1970*.
8. Houghton *1961a*; Margary *1957*, 31-2.
9. Chitty *1932*; *Britannia* v (1974), 427.
10. Rivet *1970*, 42.
11. *RIB* 2247 and 2248.
12. Margary *1957*, No. 700.
13. Houghton *1966*.
14. *NMR* 50, 5266/1 and /2.
15. Houghton *1960*.
16. St. Joseph *1965*, 85; *1973*, 235.
17. Margary *1957*, Nos. 182, 181 and 70*a*; Goodyear and Charlton *1967*.
18. Nash-Williams *1954*, 54 and fig. 62.
19. Finberg *1958*, 31.
20. Sladdin *1954*.
21. Atkinson *1942*, fig. 19.
22. Kenyon *1940*, 185, where other possibilities are also considered.
23. One regrets most the loss of *RIB* 5 with fine letters of a similar type 6 ins. high, but known only from a drawing.
24. Bushe-Fox *1913*, 21.
25. Bushe-Fox *1914*.
26. *ibid.*, fig. 19, No. 66.
27. Loeschcke *1938*; Webster and Stanley, *1964*, 116.
28. Bushe-Fox *1915*, 20-2.
29. Nash-Williams *1953*, 96; this is an oval enclosure with a wall round it with only a short length of an outer wall to suggest a bank of seats (Ashby, Hudd and Martin *1904*).
30. Some small fragments are in the Shrewsbury Museum; see also *VCH Shrops.* i, fig. 13, 229. Recent excavations here revealed fragments still *in situ*.
31. Webster *1966*.
32. The stratigraphy of the construction trenches of the two walls clearly indicates that the second stage of construction followed soon after the first, but the two walls were built of different stone, the first of red, and the encasement wall of grey, sandstone. The latter wall was finished off with a smooth mortar face about five feet above the contemporary ground level and this became totally buried and invisible to the stone robbers, who took down and

grubbed out the main walls of the baths, but left the encasement wall intact.

33. Wright *1872*, 159.
34. *ibid.*, 367.
35. Publication pending.
36. White *1936*.
37. Webster and Stanley *1964*.
38. Webster and Hollingsworth *1959*; *Trans. Shrops. Archaeol. Soc.* xlvii for 1933-4, 79.
39. It appears in *Iter II* as *Medialano* and in *Iter X* as *Mediolano*, where it is a terminal point; it is also given in the Ravenna Cosmography as *Mediolano*, No. 84, again as a terminal (Richmond and Crawford, *1949*).
40. *VCH Shrops.* i, 277.
41. Jones and Webster *1969*.
42. This assumption is based on a single pottery sherd and it is possible that this change was later.
43. A larger and more elaborate example of a *macellum* is in part of the bath *insula* at Wroxeter (fig. 23).
44. One might question whether a layer described as a 'mortar floor' (No. 25, fig. 7) was not a trampled builders' surface on which mortar was mixed.
45. This piece, No. 274, could be late third (*cf.* Frere *1972*, No. 1119, fig. 133).
46. St. Joseph *1973*, 233.
47. Gould *1964* and *1968*.
48. Rivet *1970*, 74.
49. Richmond and Crawford *1947*, 37.
50. Oswald *1968*.
51. Gould *1966*.
52. Green *1969*.
53. *Trans. North Staffs. Fld Club* xlix (1915), 139.
54. Webster *1958a*; I am grateful to Mr. A.A. Round for information on recent work on the site in advance of publication; *Britannia* v (1974), 427.
55. Webster *1971*, 42.
56. Gould *1964*, 34.
57. *ibid.*, 35.
58. Jackson *1970*, 77.
59. *ibid.*, 82.
60. St. Joseph *1958b*; Barton *1958*; Webster *1958b*.
61. Webster *1971*.

4. RURAL SETTLEMENT

1. Richmond *1963a*, 261.
2. Simpson *1962*.
3. Simpson *1964*, 142.

4. *Archaeol. Cambrensis* (1927), 333-54; (1929), 100-39; (1930), 115-30; (1932), 438-9.
5. *RIB* 430, *rivos aq]vaeductium vetus[tate conla]bs(os).*
6. Simpson *1964*, tabulated in the end paper.
7. Rivet *1955* and *1969*, fig. 5.1.
8. Phillips *1970.*
9. *CIL* xvi, 48.
10. *J. Roman Stud.* xl, (1960), No. 14, 238-9, and Thompson *1965.*
11. Watson *1969*, 148; *CAH* xi, 1936, 311.
12. *Notitia Dig.Occ.* xl, 34.
13. *VCH Shrops.* i, 258 and fig. 34.
14. *Shrops. News Letter* xl (1971), 7-10.
15. *J. Roman Stud.* xli (1951), 130; *Trans. Shrops. Archaeol. Soc.* lvi for 1957-8, 26-7.
16. *Shrops. Notes and Queries*, April, 1893.
17. *Shrops. News Letter* ii (1957); iv (1958).
18. Rainey *1973*, 167; illustrated in the *Shrops. Mag.* for Sept. 1957.
19. *Archaeologia* xxxi (1846), 339-45; *VCH Shrops.* i, 259.
20. MS Top. Salop, C.2.
21. *VCH Shrops.* i, 261. Tiles and a piece of *opus signinum* are visible in the lower herringbone courses in the north wall of the church.
22. *Trans. Shrops. Archaeol. Soc.*, 4th ser. (1911) in Miscellanea, xiii-xiv.
23. Morris *1926.*
24. Pape *1929.*
25. Goodyear *1969*; report forthcoming, *Britannia* v (1974), 426.
26. Rivet *1955.*
27. Ashcroft *1938.*
28. Wood *1961*; This name appears in the Chartulary of Haughmond Abbey, 1255.
29. Near Parlour Coppice (SO. 649926), *Shrops. News Letter* xxxviii *(1970), 19-20.*
30. Webster and Hobley *1965.*
31. *Shrops. News Letter* xxxviii (1970), 10-12.
32. *NMR* photographs SJ 3530/1-9; 3531/1; 3630/1.

5. INDUSTRY AND THE ECONOMY

1. Atkinson *1942*, 195. He suggested a name like Lucius Cornelius Hilarius.
2. Houghton *1961.*
3. This was at one time called Glevum Ware (Green *1942* and *1943*).
4. Peacock *1968*, and report forthcoming.
5. Houghton *1964.*
6. Bushe-Fox *1913*, 78.
7. Jones *1969*, No. 222-33.

8. May *1904*, 60.
9. Trinder *1973*, 214-22.
10. Cantrill *1931*.
11. Silvester *1959*.
12. Jackson *1970*, 69.
13. *Bull. of the Geological Survey of Great Britain* xiv (1958).
14. Summarised by Wright *1872*, 49-52.
15. Listed by Haverfield, *VCH Shrops.* i, 264-5; see also Webster *1953* and Whittick *1932*.
16. It is possible that the one said to have been found at Minsterley in 1857 is identical to that in the British Museum, found near Snailbeach Farm, Shropshire, in 1796-7.
17. Palmer and Ashworth *1957*.
18. Wright *1872*, 24-9.
19. According to Haverfield (*VCH Shrops.* i, 258), although Wright merely states that it was 'much thicker than the others' and it actually scales 1.65 m. on the plan, perhaps there is a transference of the number 12 which Wright gives to the wall.
20. Wright *1872*, 52-5 and *1888*; a thorough survey has been carried out by the Shropshire Mining Club and fully published with all earlier accounts, Adams *1970*.
21. Toms *1969*.
22. Atkinson *1942*, 216-18 and pl. 52.
23. As on the famous Aylesford bucket (Fox *1958*, pl. 33); for strips for other purposes see *ibid.*, pls. 34-6, 67*c*, 77 A2.
24. Bushe-Fox *1916*, 65. One of the objects, a bronze head, shows evidence of the *cire perdue* ('lost wax') process.
25. Friend and Thorneycroft *1928*; Atkinson *1942*, 226.
26. Wright *1872*, 159.
27. A good example is published by Atkinson *1942*, pl. 47, H-103.
28. I am grateful to Mr. Donald Mackreth for this information; see also his note in *Shrops. News Letter* xliv (1973), 34-5.
29. *Shrops. News Letter* xliii (1922), 15-16.

6. THE LATE FOURTH AND FIFTH CENTURIES

1. Richmond *1963a*, 62.
2. *Ammianus*, xxvii, 8; xxviii, 3.
3. This includes one in the Shrewsbury Museum, presumably found by Wright and illustrated by J. Corbet Anderson (Anderson *1867*, pl. xii) but identified as an arrowhead (*ibid.*, p. 74).
4. *De re militari*, i, 17; ii, 15.
5. Thompson *1952*, 115.
6. *Ammianus*, xxviii, 32; *in integrum restituit civitates et castra.*
7. Frere *1967*, 256-7; see also Corder *1955*, *1973*, 32, and Myres and Green *1973*, 32.
8. Baker *1971*.

9. Stevens *1941*, 134.
10. Jarrett *1968*, 90.
11. Jarrett *1964*, 61.
12. *op. cit.*, 141.
13. Frere *1967*, 362.
14. The case for this event having taken place under Maximus has been considered by Professor Alcock (Alcock *1971*, 125-9).
15. Morris *1973*, 45.
16. Wright and Jackson *1968*. The precise findspot has been re-examined by Dr A.W.J. Houghton.
17. *ibid.*, 299.
18. Barker *1971*, *1973* and *1974*; see also *Current Archaeol.* xxx (1973), 111-16.
19. Scarth *1859*, 68.
20. Gelling and Stanford *1967*, 83.
21. There is at present no secure evidence of any earlier Roman occupation of Shrewsbury. The record of Roman pottery from the Post-Office in 1880 (*VCH Shrops.* i, 276) must be regarded with suspicion; none has survived for checking and it was probably post-mediaeval. The stylus from St. Chad's crypt could have been mediaeval. The only certain Roman object is the large jar from Gallows Croft, later published by Miss L.F. Chitty (Chitty *1953*, fig. 8) with a careful consideration of the find-spot. This vessel was probably a burial along the Roman road known as the Portway and is evidence of a community here about in the late second century. Several coins have been found in different places (listed by Miss Chitty, *ibid.*, 137), most of them of fourth-century date, but the total absence of R-B pottery in the recent excavations in the town centre is surprising. As Miss Chitty suggests, this may indicate no more than a crossing-place along the river.
22. Bushe-Fox *1914*, pl. xii, fig. 2.
23. Atkinson 1942, 112-113, pl. 30b.
24. This appears to have been a widespread practice in the late Roman period and it does not signify an execution.
25. Stenton *1943*, 81.
26. A name derived from the Magnenses, that of the people living in the Roman town at Kenchester, their name in the later Roman period being applied to those of the area (Rivet *1966*, 109). The further suggestion that this tribal name is to be seen in the name of the village Maund Bryan is not the view of Ekwall, who quotes the earliest form as Magonsetum (A.D. 811) and gives *magen* as an early form of the Welsh *maen-* (stone) (Ekwall *1936*).
27. Finberg *1964*, 70-6.
28. Williams *1935*, 44.
29. Professor Melville Richards would prefer the great hall to be on the Wrekin (Richards *1973*, 142).
30. Bassa is a Saxon rather than a Celtic name but this can be explained by the fact that the geography is of Wales in the ninth century (Williams *1935*, xc-xci).

31. Richards *1973*, 143; for other views see Morris *1973*, 243, 308 and Gould *1973*.
32. *Archaeol. J.* cxiii (1957), 209.
33. Best paralled by the one at Cropthorne (Kendrick *1938*). I am grateful to Professor David Wilson for information on this point. There is another carved stone at the base of the south column of the chancel arch.

Bibliography

Adams, D.R. (1970) *Survey of Llanymynech Ogof Roman Copper Mine, Shrops. Mining Club Account* No. 8.

Alcock, L. (1971) *Arthur's Britain* (London).

Anderson, J.C. (1867) *The Roman City of Uriconium* (London).

Ashby, T., Hudd, A.E. and Martin, A.T. (1904) 'Excavations at Caerwent, Monmouthshire, on the site of the Romano-British city of Venta Silurum in the years 1901-1903', *Archaeologia* lix, 87.

Ashcroft, D. (1938) 'Report on the Roman Villa at Engleton, near Brewood', *Staffs. Record Soc.* 1938, 267.

Baker, A. (1971) 'Viroconium: A study of the defences from aerial reconnaissance', *Trans. Shrops. Archaeol. Soc.* lviii, 197.

Barker, P. (1970) 'The Origins of Worcester', *Trans. Worcs. Archaeol. Soc.* ii, 3rd. ser., 7.

Barker, P. (1971) *The Excavations on the Site of the Baths Basilica at Wroxeter, 1966-1971* (Worcester).

Barker, P. (1973) *Excavations on the Site of the Baths Basilica at Wroxeter 1972* (Worcester).

Barker, P. (1974) *Excavations on the site of the Baths Basilica at Wroxeter 1966-73* (Worcester).

Barton, I.M. (1958) 'Further excavations at *Pennocrucium*, near Stretton Bridge, 1953-4', *Trans. Birmingham Archaeol. Soc.* lxxiv, 6.

Birley, E. (1953) *Roman Britain and the Roman Army* (Kendal).

Bushe-Fox, J.P. (1913) *Excavations on the Site of the Roman Town at Wroxeter, Shropshire, in 1912* (London).

Bushe-Fox, J.P. (1914) *Second Report on the Excavations on the Site of the Roman Town at Wroxeter, Shropshire, 1913* (London).

Bushe-Fox, J.P. (1916) *Third Report on the Excavations on the Site of the Roman Town at Wroxeter, Shropshire, 1914* (London).

Cantrill, T.C. (1931) 'Geological report on Uriconium', *Archaeol. Camb.* lxxxvi, 87-98.

Chadwick, H.M. (1954) *Studies in Early British History* (London).

Chitty, L.F. (1927a) 'Dug-out canoes from Shropshire', *Trans. Shrops. Archaeol. Soc.* xliv, 113.

Chitty, L.F. (1927b) 'Prehistoric Shropshire', *Trans. Shrops. Archaeol. Soc.* xliv, 113.

Chitty, L.F. (1932) 'Proceedings', *Trans. Shrops. Archaeol. Soc.* xlvi, x.

Chitty, L.F. (1953) 'Prehistoric and other early finds in the borough of Shrewsbury', *Trans. Shrops. Archaeol. Soc.* liv, 105.

Chitty, L.F. (1963) 'Clun-Clee Ridgeway', in Foster and Alcock *1963*, 171.

Corder, P. (1955) 'The reorganisation of the defences of Romano-British towns in the fourth century', *Archaeol. J.* cxii, 20.

Crawford, O.G.S. (1954) 'Celtic Fields on the Long Mynd', *Antiquity* xxviii, 168.

Cunliffe, Barry (1973) *The Regni* (London).

Curle, James (1911) *A Roman Frontier Post and its People; The Fort at Newstead in the Parish of Melrose* (Glasgow).

Dury, G. (1959) *The Face of the Earth* (Harmondsworth, Middlesex).

Ekwall, E. (1936) *The Concise Dictionary of English Place-Names* (London).

Finberg, H.P.R. (1958) 'Three Anglo-Saxon charters', *Trans. Shrops. Archaeol. Soc.* lvi, 28.

Finberg, H.P.R. (1964) *Lucerna* (London).

Foster, I.Ll. and Alcock, L. (ed.) (1963) *Culture and Environment* (London).

Fox, C. (1958) *Pattern and Purpose* (Cardiff).

Fox, G.E. (1897) 'Uriconium', *Archaeol. J.* liv, 123.

Frere, S.S. (ed.) (1959) *Problems of the Iron Age in Southern Britain* (London).

Frere, S.S. (1967) *Britannia* (London).

Frere, S.S. (1972) *Verulamium* I (London).

Friend, J.A.N. and Thorneycroft, N.E. (1928) 'An example of Roman copper soldering', *J. Inst. Metals* xxxlx, 61.

Forster, R.H. and Knowles, W.H. (1915) 'Corstopitum: report on the excavations in 1914', *Archaeol. Aeliana*, 3rd ser., xii, 227.

Gelling, P.S. (1959) 'Excavations at Caynham Camp, near Ludlow', First Interim Report, *Trans. Shrops. Archaeol. Soc.* lvi, 145.

Gelling, P.S. (1964) 'Excavations at Caynham Camp, near Ludlow', *Trans. Shrops. Archaeol. Soc.* lvii, 91.

Gelling, P.S. and Peacock, D.P.S. (1968) 'The pottery from Caynham Camp, near Ludlow' *Trans. Shrops. Archaeol. Soc.* lviii, 96.

Gelling, P.S. and Stanford, S.C. (1967) 'Dark Age pottery and Iron Age ovens', *Trans. Birmingham Archaeol. Soc.* lxxxii, 77.

Goodyear, F.H. (1969) 'The Roman villa site at Hales, Staffs: an interim report', *N. Staffs. J. of Fld. Stud.* ix, 104.

Goodyear, F.H. and Charlton, J.M.T. (1967) 'A Roman road in North Staffordshire', *N. Staffs. J. of Fld. Stud.* vii, 27.

Gould, J. (1964) 'Excavations at Wall 1961-3', *Trans. Lichfield and S. Staffs. Archaeol and Hist. Soc.* v, 1.

Gould, J. (1966) 'Excavations in advance of road construction between Shenstone and Wall', *Trans. Lichfield and S. Staffs. Archaeol. and Hist. Soc.* vi, 1.

Gould, J. (1968) 'Excavations at Wall, Staffs, 1964-6, on the site of the Roman Fort', *Trans. Lichfield and S. Staffs. Archaeol. Hist. Soc.* viii, 1.

Gould, J. (1973) 'Letocetum, Christianity and Lichfield (Staffs.)', *Trans. S. Staffs. Archaeol. and Hist. Soc.* xiv, 30.

Green, C. (1943) 'Glevum and the Second Legion', *J. Roman Stud.* xxxiii, 15.

Green, M. (1969) 'Godmanchester', *Current Archaeol* xvi, 133.

Hartley, B.R. (1952) 'Excavations at Heronbridge, 1947-48', *J. Chester and N. Wales Archaeol. Soc.* xxxix, 3.

Hartley, B.R. (1964) 'A bronze-worker's hearth', *J. Chester and N. Wales Archaeol. Soc.* xli, 15.

Hartley, B.R. (1966) 'Dating town buildings and structures', in Wacher, J.S. (ed.) *The Civitas Capitals of Roman Britain* (Leicester), 52.

Hartley, B.R. (1971) 'The Roman occupation of Scotland; the evidence of the samian ware', *Britannia* iii, 1.

Hawkes, C.F.C. (1959) 'The ABC of the British Iron Age', in Frere, S.S. (ed.) (*1959*), 1.

Houghton, A.W.J. (1960) 'The Roman road from Greensforge through the Central Welsh March', *Trans. Shrops. Archaeol. Soc.* lvi, 223.

Houghton, A.W.J. (1961a) 'The Roman road from Wroxeter to Whitchurch (Salop)', *N. Staffs. J. Fld. Stud.* i, 51.

Houghton, A.W.J. (1961b) 'A Roman tilery and brickfield at Ismore Coppice, Wroxeter', *Trans. Shrops. Archaeol. Soc.* lvii, 7.

Houghton, A.W.J. (1964) 'A Roman pottery factory near Wroxeter, Salop', *Trans. Shrops. Archaeol. Soc.* lvii, 101.

Houghton, A.W.J. (1966) 'A Roman road from Ashton, N. Hereford-shire to Marshbrook, Salop', *Trans. Shrops. Archaeol. Soc.* lvii, 185.

Hurst, H. (1972) 'Excavations at Gloucester 1968-71', *Antiq. J.* lii, 24.

Jackson, K.H. (1953) *Language and History in Early Britain* (Edinburgh).

Jackson, K.H. (1970) 'Romano-British names in the Antonine Itinerary', Appendix II to Rivet *1970*, 68.

Jarrett, M.G. (1964) 'Legio II Augusta in Britain', *Archaeol. Cambrensis* cxiii, 47.

Jarrett, M.G. (1968) 'Legio XX Valeria Victrix in Britain', *Archaeol. Cambrensis* cxvii, 77.

Jarrett, M.G. and Mann, J.C. (1968) 'The tribes of Wales', *Welsh Hist. Rev.* iv, 161.

Jarrett, M.G. and Mann, J.C. (1970) 'Britain from Agricola to Gallienus', *Bonner Jahrb.* clxx, 178.

Jones, G.D.B. (1972) 'Excavations at Northwich', *Archaeol. J.* cxxviii, 31.

Jones, G.D.B. and Webster, P.V. (1969) 'Mediolanum: excavations at Whitchurch 1965-6', *Archaeol. J.* cxxv, 193.

Kendrick, T.D. (1938) *Anglo-Saxon Art to A.D. 900* (London).

Kenyon, K.M. (1940) 'Excavations at Viroconium, 1936-7', *Archaeologia* lxxxviii, 175.

Kenyon, K.M. (1943) 'Excavations on the Wrekin, Shropshire, 1939', *Archaeol. J.* xcix, 99.

Lewis, N. and Reinhold, M. (1955) *Roman Civilisation* (New York).

Loeschcke, S. (1938) *Der Tempelbezirk im Altbachtale zu Trier* I (Berlin).

Lynch, F. and Burgess, C. (ed.) (1972) *Prehistoric Man in Wales and the West* (Bath).

MacMullen, R. (1963) *'Soldiers and Civilian in the Later Roman Empire* (Cambridge, Mass.).

Mahany, C. (1971) 'Excavations at Manduessedum 1964', *Trans. Birmingham Archaeol. Soc.* lxxxiv, 18.

Margary, I.D. (1957) *Roman Roads in Britain* (London).

May, T. (1904) *Warrington's Roman Remains* (Warrington).

Meeson, R.A. (1966) 'A Section across Watling Street at Overley Hill, near Wellington', *Trans. Shrops. Archaeol. Soc.* lviii, 111.

Mócsy, A. (1953) *'Das Territorium legionis und die Canabae in Pannonien'*, *Acta Arch. Acad. Scient. Hungaricae* iii, 179.

Mócsy, A. (1967) *'Zu den Prata legionis'*, *Studien zu den Militärgrenzen Roms.*, 211 (Köln).

Morris, J. (1973) *The Age of Arthur* (London).

Morris, J.A. (1926) 'Excavations at Stow, Shrops.', *Trans. Shrops. Archaeol. Soc.* x (1925-6), iv.

Musson, C. (1972) 'Two winters at the Breiddin', *Current Archaeol.* xxxiii, 263.

Myres, J.L. and Green, C. (1973) *The Anglo-Saxon Cemeteries of Caistor-by-Norwich and Marleshall.*

Nash-Williams, V.E. (1953) 'The forum and basilica and public baths of the Roman town of Venta Silurum at Caerwent in Monmouthshire' *Bull. Board Celtic Stud.* xv, 159.

Nash-Williams, V.E. (1954) *The Roman Frontier in Wales.* (Cardiff).

O'Neil, B.H. St. J. (1934) 'Excavations at Titterstone Clee Hill Camp, Shropshire, 1932', *Antiq. J.* xiv, 13.

O'Neil, B.H. St. J. (1937) 'Excavations at Breiddin Hill Camp, Montgomeryshire, 1933-5', *Archaeol. Cambrensis* xcii, 86.

Oswald, A. (1968) 'Observation on the construction of the by-pass road at Wall, Staffs, *Trans. Lichfield and S. Staffs. Archaeol. and Hist. Soc.* viii, 39.

Palmer, L.S. and Ashworth, H.W.W. (1957) 'Four Roman pigs of lead from the Mendips', *Proc. Somerset Archaeol. Natur. Hist. Soc.* ci/cii, 52.

Pape, T. (1929) 'Roman discoveries at Hales', *Trans. No. Staffs. Fld. Club* lxiii, 98.

Pauly-Wissowa-Kroll, (1894-1972) *Realencyclopädie der Klassischen Altentumswissenschaft* (Stuttgart).

Peacock, D.P.S. (1968) 'Romano-British pottery production in the Malvern district', *Trans. Worcs. Archaeol. Soc.* 3rd ser., i. 15.

Peacock, D.P.S. (1969) 'A petrological study of certain Iron Age pottery from Western England', *Proc. Prehist. Soc.* xxxiv, 414.

Phillips, C.W. (1970) *The Fenland in Roman Times* (Royal Geographical Society).

Rainey, A. (1973) *Mosaics in Roman Britain* (Newton Abbott).

Richards, M. (1973) 'The 'Lichfield' Gospels (Book of Saint Chad)', *Nat. Library of Wales J.* xviii, 135.

Richmond, I.A. (1950) 'Excavations at the Roman fort of Newstead, 1947' *Proc. Soc. Antiq. Scot.* lxxiv, 1.

Richmond, I.A. (1963a) 'The Cornovii', in Foster and Alcock *1963*, 251.

Richmond, I.A. (1963b) *Roman Britain*, 2nd ed.

Richmond, I.A. and Crawford, O.G.S. (1949) 'The British section of the Ravenna Cosmography', *Archaeologia* xciii, 1.

Richmond, I.A. and Ogilvie, R.M. (1967) *De Vita Agricolae* (London).

Richmond, I.A. and Webster, G. (1950) 'The excavations at Goss St., Chester, 1948-9', *Chester Archaeol. Soc. J.*, xxxviii, 1.

Rivet, A.L.F. (1955) 'The distribution of Roman villas in Britain', in *Romano-British Villas: some current problems*, C.B.A. Research Report No. 1.

Rivet, A.L.F. (ed.) (1969) *The Roman Villa in Britain* (London).

Rivet, A.L.F. (1970) 'The British Section of the Antonine Itinerary', *Britannia* i, 34.

Ross, A. (1967) *Pagan Celtic Britain* (London).

St. Joseph, J.K. (1953a) 'Roman forts on Watling Street near Penkridge and Wroxeter', *Trans. Birmingham Archaeol. Soc.* lxix, 50.

St. Joseph, J.K. (1953b) 'Air reconnaissance of Southern Britain' *J. Roman Stud.* xliii, 81.

St. Joseph, J.K. (1958a) 'Air reconnaissance in Britain, 1955-7' *J. Roman Stud.* xlviii, 86.

St. Joseph, J.K. (1958b) 'The Roman site near Stretton Bridge, the ancient Pennocrucium', *Trans. Birmingham Archaeol. Soc.* lxxiv, 1.

St. Joseph, J.K. (1961) 'Air reconnaissance in Britain 1958-1960', *J. Roman Stud.* li, 199.

St. Joseph, J.K. (1965) 'Air reconnaissance in Britain, 1961-64', *J. Roman Stud.* lv, 74.

St. Joseph, J.K. (1969) 'Air reconnaissance in Britain, 1965-68', *J. Roman Stud.* lix, 104.

St. Joseph, J.K. (1973) 'Air reconnaissance in Britain, 1969-72', *J. Roman Stud.* lxiii, 214.

Scarth, Rev. H.M. (1859) 'Notices of Wroxeter, the Roman Uriconium in Shropshire', *Archaeol. J.* xvi, 53.

Scott, K. (1973) 'A section across the defences of a Roman fort at Mancetter, Warks', *Trans. Birmingham Archaeol. Soc.* lxxxv, 211.

Silvester, W.A. (1959) 'Wroxeter and Yarchester — stone shingle roofing', *Shrops. Newsletter*, ix, 3.

Simpson, G. (1962) 'Caerleon and the Roman forts in Wales in the Second Century A.D.', *Archaeol. Camb.* cxi, 103.

Simpson, G. (1964) *Britons and the Roman Army* (London).

Sladdin, E. (1954) 'Acton Burnell Roman road and bridge site', *Trans. Shrops. Archaeol. Soc.* lv, 38.

Spurgeon, C.J. (1972) 'Enclosures of the Iron Age type in the Upper Severn Basin', in Lynch, F. and Burgess, C. *1972*, 331.

Stanford, S.C. (1967) 'Croft Ambrey hill-fort', *Trans. Woolhope Nat. Fld. Club* xxxix, 31.

Stanford, S.C. (1968) 'The Roman forts at Leintwardine and Buckton', *Trans. Woolhope Fld. Club* xxxix, 222.

Stanford, S.C. (1971) 'Credenhill Camp, Herefordshire: an Iron Age hill-fort capital', *Archaeol. J.* cxxviii, 82.

Stanford, S.C. (1972a) 'Welsh Border forts', *The Iron Age in the Irish Sea Province* (CBA Research Report No. 9), 25.

Stanford, S.C. (1972b) 'The function and population of hill-forts in the central marches' in Lynch, F. and Burgess, C. *1972*, 307.

Stanford, S.C. (1974) *Croft Ambrey* (Leominster).

Stenton, F.M. (1943) *Anglo-Saxon England* (London).

Stevens, C.E. (1941) 'The British sections of the Notitia Dignitatum', *Archaeol. J.* xcvii, 125.

Thomas, C. (1963) 'The animal art of the Scottish Iron Age and its origins', *Archaeol. J.* cxviii, 14.

Thompson, E.A. (1952) *A Roman Reformer and Inventor* (London).

Thompson, F.H. (1959) *Deva* (Chester).

Thompson, F.H. (1965) *Roman Cheshire* (Chester).

Toms, G. (1969) 'Excavations at Llanymynech', *Shrops. News Letter* xxxvi, 20.

Trinder, B. (1973) *The Industrial Revolution in Shropshire* (London and Chichester).

Varley, W.J. (1950) 'The hill-forts of the Welsh Marches' *Archaeol. J.* cv, 41.

Wacher, J. (1964) 'A survey of Romano-British town defences of the early and middle second century', *Archaeol. J.* cxix, 103.

Walker, C.I. (1967) 'Excavations at the Roman fort at Walltown Farm, Shropshire, 1960-1', *Trans. Shrops. Archaeol. Soc.* lviii, 8.

Waters, P.L. (1963) 'A Romano-British tile kiln at Upper Sandlin Farm, Leigh Sinton, Worcs.', *Trans. Worcs. Archaeol. Soc.* xl, 1.

Watson, G.R. (1969) *The Roman Soldier* (London).

Webster, G. (1953) 'The lead-mining industry in North Wales in Roman times', *Flintshire Hist. Soc.* xiii, 3.

Webster, G. (1958) 'The bath-house at Wall, Staffs., excavations in 1956', *Trans. Birmingham Archaeol. Soc.* lxxiv, 12.

Webster, G. (1958) 'Road-widening at *Pennocrucium* in 1956; a note', *Trans. Birmingham Archaeol. Soc.* lxxiv, 10.

Webster, G. (1959) 'A note on the Roman coin hoard found at Hordley Grange', *Trans. Shrops. Archaeol. Soc.* lvi, 138.

Webster, G. (1962) 'The defences of Viroconium (Wroxeter)', *Trans. Birmingham Archaeol. Soc.* lxxviii, 27.

Webster, G. (1964a) 'Wroxeter', *Current Archaeol.* xiv, 82.

Webster, G. (1964b) 'Roman finds from Red Hill, near Oakengates', *Trans. Shrops. Archaeol. Soc.* lvii, 132.

Webster, G. (1971) 'A Roman system of fortified posts along Watling

Street', *Roman Frontier Studies 1967* (Tel Aviv).

Webster, G. and Daniels, C. (1972) 'A street section at Wroxeter in 1962', *Trans. Shrops. Archaeol. Soc.* lix, 15.

Webster, G. and Dudley, D.R. (1962) *The Rebellion of Boudicca* (London).

Webster, G. and Dudley, D.R. (1973) *The Roman Conquest of Britain*, 2nd. ed. (London).

Webster, G. and Hobley, B. (1965) 'Aerial reconnaissance over the Warwickshire Avon', *Archaeol. J.* cxxi, 1.

Webster, G. and Hollingsworth, D. (1959) 'The Wroxeter aqueduct', *Trans. Shrops. Archaeol. Soc.* lvi, 133.

Webster, G. and Stanley, B. (1964) 'Viroconium: a study of problems', *Trans. Shrops. Archaeol. Soc.* lvii, 112.

Webster, G. and Woodfield, P. (1966) 'The "Old Work" at the Roman public baths at Wroxeter', *Antiq. J.* xlvi, 229.

Wheeler, R.E.M. (1954) *The Stanwick Fortifications* (London).

White, G.M. (1936) 'The Chichester amphitheatre: preliminary excavations', *Antiq. J.* xvi, 149.

Whittick, G.C. (1932) 'The Shropshire pigs of lead', *Trans. Shrops. Archaeol. Soc.* xlvi, 129.

Williams, I. (1935) *Canu Llywarch Hen* (London).

Wood, J. (1961) 'The site of Stanchester', *Trans. Shrops. Archaeol. Soc.* lvii, 13.

Wright, R.P. and Jackson, K.H. (1968) 'A late inscription from Wroxeter', *Antiq. J.* xlviii, 296.

Wright, T. (1872) *Uriconium* (London).

Wright, T. (1888) 'Roman mining operations in Shropshire and North Wales', *Trans. Shrops. Archaeol. Soc.* xi, 272.

Glossary of Latin Terms

adiutrix a title given to legions (e.g. *Legio II Adiutrix*), meaning raised originally as a reserve force.

agger the bank on which a road was constructed for drainage and easing gradients. In Britain they normally belong to the economic development of the Province in the early second century.

agger publicus populi Romani land taken into public ownership, normally by conquest.

ala literally a wing, the name given to a cavalry regiment of 500 (or 1,000) horsemen, the senior of the auxiliary formations.

annona the yearly corn tax imposed on provinces for supplying the army. Farmers were obliged to transport the grain to chosen centres, even to the forts themselves, a serious grievance in Britain in the first century.

auxilia palatina units of the field army created in the earth fourth century and originally attached to the emperors.

beneficiarius a long-serving soldier seconded for special duties, often of a civil character, including customs and tax collecting, policing areas or acting as a kind of district officer.

burgus from the Greek word for a tower, applied to small fortifications along main routes in the third and fourth centuries.

canabae literally huts, a name given to the settlements outside the gates of the legionary fortress. They housed the taverns, brothels, shops and places of amusement for the troops and were under military control.

caldarium the very hot room in the steam-heated section of a bath-house. It usually included a hot bath built over the furnace, and alcoves where bathers could sit and be cleansed and massaged.

catena a chain; applied also to fetters and slave chains, hence the sobriquet given to the notorious Paul, sent to Britain in the mid-fourth century to round up the followers of Magnentius.

civium Romanorum a title given to an auxiliary unit, all the soldiers of which had been given citizenship while serving, as recognition of meritorious service. Normally citizenship was given only on satisfactory service and honorary discharge.

civitas a term used of a tribe and embracing all its people and its chief city, a concept which has no British parallel.

cohors an auxiliary unit of 500 to 1,000 men.

colonia a settlement for retired army veterans with land grants in the area (*territorium*) around, the plots often laid out on a carefully surveyed grid, although no examples of this have yet been noticed in Britain where there were three *coloniae*, Camulodunum, Londinium and Glevum. It was also an honour given to an existing city, as in the case of the civil settlement at York.

damnatio most emperors were given divine status after death, with appropriate ceremonies, including the release of an eagle from the funeral pyre to symbolise the spirit of the man aspiring to the heavens. An unpopular emperor could be as easily be damned and his spirit consigned elsewhere; his name was then erased from inscriptions all over the Empire. It was a fate accorded to Domitian and unscrupulously to Geta by his brother, Caracalla.

denarius a silver coin rather smaller but thicker than a 5p piece. There were 25 to the *aureus* (gold) and it was equal to four *sestertii*.

diplomata the discharge certificate required by a retired auxiliary for proof of his citizenship. It took the form of a pair of bronze plates, and the lettering chiselled on the surface gives the man's name, his unit, and other units which were discharging veterans on that occasion in the province. They provide us with considerable army lists and are recorded in a special volume of *CIL*, xiv.

forum a public building in the centre of a city which included a large colonnaded market, basilicar hall for meetings, law courts and a suite of administrative offices.

frigidarium the cold room of a bath-house, which included a cold bath for feet washing and cold sluicing.

in castris a term aplied to children born outside the forts to soldiers, who were not allowed to marry while serving, but contracted unions with the expectation of a legal contract on discharge.

insula an island; applied to the blocks of land in the street grid of a city.

iter a road or route, hence our word itinerary.

laconicum a room in a bath-house which had dry heat; there were usually two, of different temperatures. Known also as a *sudatorium* (sweating room).

legio a unit of about 5,000 heavily armoured infantry, all Roman citizens. The force of almost twenty *legiones* formed the backbone of the Roman army in the first two centuries of the empire.

legatus augusti a legate appointed by the Emperor, as in the case of the governor of a province; a *legatus legionis* was a legionary commander.

macellum a small market, usually found only in the larger cities.

mansio a hostelry established along the main routes to provide travellers with food and accommodation. They were normally at about twenty-mile intervals, with *mutationes* (relay-stations) between.

martiobarbulus a pottery mixing bowl, the interior studded with grits to facilitate pulverising, and with a pouring spout. It was usual in Britain for the potters to stamp their name on each side of the spout, or to stamp their name on one side and FECIT (made it) on the other.

municipium a city honoured with municipal status equivalent to that of a *colonia.* It had an *ordo* (city council), magistrates and a fair amount of self-government.

opus signinum a cement flooring which was compounded of small pieces of broken tile which had the effect of making it waterproof, hence its use in bath-houses.

ordo the city council, usually of about one hundred members, from which the senior and junior magistrates were elected.

palaestra an open colonnaded area, especially that attached to a bath-house where bathers could exercise themselves before their bath. They were part of the early bath-house in Britain (as at Wroxeter), but it was soon found that the weather necessitated an enclosed building, and they were then converted into *basilicae.*

plumbata a short javelin weighted with lead and used in the fourth century by infantry with effect against cavalry. It became the weapon of some of the legions and the *auxilia palatina*, which were given the honorific title *martiobarbulus.*

piscina a large pool normally in the open and associated with a bath-house. Its function is purely ornamental and, as at Wroxeter, it is usually found in a colonnaded area; it is not to be confused with a *natatio* or swimming-pool, or with the cold plunge in the *frigidarium.*

praefurnium the stoke area of a bath-house.

praetorium the name given to the house of the unit commander in a fort or fortress; but it could also apply to the administrative office of an imperial estate.

principia the headquarters building in a fort or fortress, occuping a central position.

procurator a civil servant responsible for administration and finance in the provinces. The senior post was that of finance officer. Although below the governor, he was nevertheless directly responsible to the Emperor. Other posts were connected with mines, salt-works etc.

quaestorius a man with the duties of a *quaestor*, who was a junior magistrate responsible for local taxes and revenue.

taberna a place where strong drinks could be consumed.

territorium the area or town around a military establishment, over which the army or civil authority had some legal control.

tepidarium the warm room in the wet suite of a bath-house, between the *frigidarium* and the *caldarium.*

tessera a small piece of stone, glass or tile, square in section, for a mosaic or tessellated pavement.

thermae a large bath-house; usually applied to those in cities.

tria nomina the three names, *praenomen, nomen* and *cognomen*, usually given to a Roman citizen, they appear with his birthplace, tribal affiliation and father's name in official documents and on tombstones. Some citizens have more than three names.

via praetoria the street in a fort or fortress at right-angles to the *via principalis*, which led to the gate in front of the entrance to the *principia.*

via principalis the street across the centre of a fort or fortress, running in front of the *principia.*

victrix literally victorious, a honorific term given to legions which had won important battles, e.g. *Legio XX Valeria Victrix*.

vicus a unit of local government, as applied to a town or settlement below the rank of a *colonia* and a *municipium* and with a certain degree of local autonomy. The term can also apply to part of a large city (similar to a ward).

Index